Praise for]

"While the shocking events ᴏꜰ David's ꜱᴛᴏʀy will have you captivated, his struggle to find strength in his faith and the many miraculous moments that cross his path will leave you inspired. Peppered with David's witty self-awareness and humility, the book will have you wanting much more!"

Community Phone Company Newsletter –

Cambridge, Massachusetts 9/18/2018

*****

"Dear Brother in Christ, Thank you for sharing your life in written word. I look forward to each post. I am looking forward to the book. I am anxiously waiting to sit and read it straight through with no interruptions! Your writings are an inspiration and so helpful!!"

C. H. McNeair – Georgia

*****

"There are so many you are helping with your journey through life. You are a blessing to many!"

Ramona Moyes – North Dakota

*****

"Excellence!!!! Beautiful disciple of Yeshua!"

Anita Landoll – Virginia

*****

"His touch is more precious than anything else in existence … Amazing story!"

Justin Fowler – Washington

"Absolutely the truth! I am very thankful I read one of your posts a little over a year ago and have followed ever since. I more than likely wouldn't be where I am today. I give all the credit to God for sending you to me (via Facebook) and thankful that something in me told me to read it!"

Wendy Durham – Tennessee

*****

"Such a heartfelt post. I always appreciate how real this page is … it has made me dig deeper into my faith journey, pray more, pray for others more, be more intentional about what I do, and what I pray!"

Lori MacMillan

*****

"I have been impacted by you, as a guy, just a guy, talking about God. It's easier to learn from plain people. That sounds like a putdown, lol, but it's a compliment!"

F. Harasimiw – Ontario

*****

"Thank you, David. This is mind-boggling, really. I have taken, or rather stolen, some content that I will later use … thank you in advance! And indeed, you are a word guy!"

Peter Moleke – South Africa

the Baker

Prelude to a New Kind of Life

David W. Riordan

GreenTree Publishers

Newnan, GA

The Baker –
Prelude to a New Kind of Life

ISBN: 978-1-944483-35-7

Cover Design By: Justin Fowler
Visit JustinFowlerDesign.com for more
information on Justin's work.

Published by GreenTree Publishers,
Newnan, GA – greentreepublishers.com

Dedication

I dedicate this book to the Baker—my Lord
and Savior Jesus Christ.

And to my mother, who swore God told her I
would be a preacher one day.

For now, these pages are my pulpit,
the streets, my congregation.

May the telling of my story bring Glory to
God and relief to battered souls!

Contents

Acknowledgements

I do not know where to begin. There are hundreds of people who have poured effort into the success of this book and its partner, my blog, the Baker and the Bread on Facebook.

I thank them all.

Specifically, this work would not have gotten off the ground without Thomas and Bessie, Cathy, Kate, Elizabeth, and Tom in Massachusetts. In the beginning, they all believed in the work God was doing in my life and have supported me. I would not be where I am without God's work through them.

In Texas, I have my friend Cliff, Beth, Thomas, Clarlyn, Jim, Scott, Kelly, and my pastor, Cole.

Georgia is where most of my family resides, and wow! What a tremendous influence and help they have been. Thanks to Tim and his publishing efforts through GreenTree Publishers, Rebecca, and Dad! And, of course, my nephew Timothy for his contributions to both the soundtrack and the book trailers.

And, all by herself over in Uganda, Esther has put together a fantastic effort to reach people around her through this book and my blog. The Swahili translation would not have happened without her!

Finally, how do you thank a guy who reads your book and is inspired to compose a soundtrack? The Lord works through my brother, Dan. He is my encourager, my shoulder, my brother, and my friend.

And, well, I still owe him $15.00.

About the Music

Download or listen to the Prelude Soundtrack included with your purchase at:
DavidWRiordan.com/soundtrack.

From the Author

In December 2019, I began working again on the manuscript for my whole story, the Baker. God sat me down. It was time to finish.

However, I had to start with a rewrite of what was the Baker – Prelude. The story had not changed, but I needed to make it better. As I was writing, I received a phone call from Dan, my brother, who is a composer.

"Dave, have you considered a soundtrack for the book?"

Who would have ever thought of such a thing? "Musical tracks for a book?"

My first thoughts were music to play along as you read. I sent a copy of the manuscript to Dan that had approximately 240 words per page because that is how fast the average person reads in a minute.

Dan is far wiser than I. "Dave, listening to music while you read will distract from the story, and people need the message of your book. What I want to do is write music that sets the mood for portions of the story—lay the foundation emotionally and spiritually through music before they read that section. It will go with the book, but not simultaneous to reading."

And he did it!

What a tremendous job! Stylistically, there may be some music to which you are not used to listening. There is variety in the soundtrack, and I encourage you to hear it all. Follow the suggestions in the book as you read along.

Rounding out Dan's composition efforts are contributions of another family member, my nephew, Timothy Riordan, and his band, Atlas Rhoads.

I can claim nothing for the music other than being a fan. What Dan, Timothy, and I have done together with God's leading is to create something that goes beyond a typical reading experience.

Some of the notes are written by Dan and Timothy, and some are by me. Feel free to add your own!

With their musical genius, Dan and Timothy have reached deep inside the essence of the story, wrestled from it the raw emotion and spirit, molding them into a sensory experience that speaks to the soul in a way words alone cannot.

Track 1: Helper

April 22, 2018—I don't know that I will ever forget the feeling of desperation that washed over me as I stood on the edge of US 19/41, gazing north. Almost without hope, I put one foot into Malier Road. In my mind, as I remember that step, I can hear that bass note sounding at the beginning of this song with the melancholy vocal coming in.

Desperation and Darkness.

The light at the end of the tunnel was not yet in my vision.

But, it was apparent to me and everyone around me that I could not do this on my own!

"So you should look for the LORD before it is too late. You should call to Him now, while He is near."
Isaiah 55:6 (ERV)

Foreword

In my many years of ministering to the down and out, I have heard a lot of people's stories. When this scruffy-looking fellow from our shelter approached me about attending our church services, I heard him out. He told me, with his country twang on fast forward, of his commitment to being obedient to God's leading. Even though I had heard similar stories many times before, when he began telling me his story, I was mesmerized. Whether it was his southern charm, his sincere heart, or the Spirit working through him, I was interested in what he had to say.

I told him the time our services began, and he actually showed up. He continued to show up faithfully. Soon he started telling me of his desire to worship God through music. I informed him that he could have access to the piano. This enabled me to talk with David more often. Slowly his story unfolded, and I couldn't help but feel compassion for him.

Eventually, he told me he was writing his story, and I asked him if I could read it. He agreed and gave me the first chapter, and I was hooked. He continued giving me more chapters. It was an incredible story that explained what brought about the faithfulness and obedience I had been seeing lived out in David's life. I realized that his tears, fears, and struggles about which we had talked only scratched the surface of what he had gone through.

With eloquence and wit, David has laid out his heart-wrenching story. I think it is a journey to which a vast majority of people can relate. Discovering the road he has traveled and his perseverance through trials will encourage anyone who has been there.

Read a few pages, and you will, without question, be eager to read one more page.

Thomas S. Babbitt, Major
The Salvation Army Cambridge, MA

To M

And everyone like her who simply wants to know my Father as I do.

Track 2: Escape

I had to leave. There was no doubt. However, running away is not synonymous with escaping.

Ask the former resident of the frying pan.

It is not only necessary to know what or where you are leaving, but the direction you must go to escape, as well.

I didn't have a clue as to where, but I did know to Whom I should run.

Partially written in Dorian mode, the hearer has difficulty determining in what key this piece is written. However, as in my story, if you pay close attention, with the uncertainty, and the unsettling need to go, you will also find the journey of discovery, and victories along the way. Perhaps you will hear the rain and the proverbial mountains I had to climb. Surely, you will detect the relief of an answer received.

"I run for dear life to God, and I'll never live to regret it. Do what You do so well: get me out of this mess and up on my feet!" Psalm 71:1, 2 (MSG)

1

Ingredients

"Drop me off at the RaceTrac," I said with all the confidence I did not feel. I had no choice. Behind me lay sorrow, pain, addiction, destruction, and death. Ahead of me—not a clue. Funny how several people have praised me recently about that step of faith. In reality, I had no choice, no real choice, at any rate.

"Surely, I can find a ride out of this place" (one of the busiest gas stations in my hometown of Griffin, Georgia).

I was wrong.

As I gazed to the north, my intended egress, I saw nothing but heavy overcast, black clouds in mid-afternoon, belying even the existence of the sun, and seeking to erase any glimmer of hope that might exist deep inside me. But as I said, I had no real choice. No choice, I have discovered, is, after all, a great motivator in my life.

Into the gloom, I walked, and it started to rain. Not much rain. Just a constant drizzle. Enough to be uncomfortable—certainly not enough to make me turn around.

If I had only known!

So, I walked and walked. Two things were swirling in my head. One—one of my favorite songs, Keith Green's "O Lord You're Beautiful." Two—my spoken refusal to God to curse Him because of my misery and die.

Not that I, in any shape, form, or fashion, claimed to be Job. I certainly had had some misery and loss in my life. After all, I was leaving my hometown, never to return, with work boots on my feet, jeans, shirt and leather jacket on my back–and the fifteen dollars my brother had just given me.

"Now, Dave, I am not giving this to you to encourage you to leave. I think you should stay and face your problems," he said.

Of course, he had not had three recent attempts on his life.

Now, I don't get queasy at the sight of my blood. Thirty years of construction experience have taught me that "if I don't see a little of my blood every day, I ain't workin'!" One of my oft repeated, if not necessarily world-famous mantras. That being said, I sincerely did not wish to see my life's blood flowing out through a small round hole.

I had to leave. That made me miserable. Leaving underscored all the things and people I had lost in my life and highlighted the fact that it was my fault. I didn't dodge my own bullets or duck my own knife, but I had made choices. At the time, I felt they were not wrong choices, but decisions with consequences. One of those nasty things about life, choices equal consequences. I had made choices in the previous year with admirable intentions. However, we all know what paves the road to Hell.

I am not a stupid man, despite what some may think. I understood precisely what the outcome of those decisions might be. I was not in the least caught off guard, for every gambler knows he may lose it all. Every rock climber knows he may fall, and every builder knows there is always a risk when he uses seconds.

The consequences could be catastrophic.

I've done all three. I, like most risk takers, view myself as a winner.

Denial equals strength?

Well, at least it shields us from pessimism.

I have also faced catastrophic consequences and still managed to survive.

Survival equals winning?

I admit it. I don't always think the way everyone else does. I view things a little differently—

no, scratch that—

a lot differently. I will go ahead and give you a spoiler. I am wrong sometimes—

no, scratch that—

often.

I needed to have a conversation with my Father. You know, one of those conversations you have as you are beginning to mature in life. The kind where you own up to something.

"Dad, I wrecked the car."

"Dad, I need you to bond me out of jail."

"Dad, I don't have a bond this time. I need you to take care of some things for me."

The kind of conversation where you admit you're wrong because you don't have any other reasonable choice, and you realize it—the kind where there is no one else to blame.

"Father, I am in a bind."

I could spiritually hear His response, "Boy, that don't take a rocket scientist to figure out."

"Yeah, I know. It is all my fault. I know you set me up with a task, and I accepted willingly, even excitedly."

"I knew you would. After all, I'm kinda in the position where I actually do know everything, but Dave, why didn't you stick to the script?"

"Well, Father, I was excited and walked out of the room before I even read the script. I went out there on my own. I was so intrigued by the job offer."

"Look, Dave, I know you. I knew you needed a script. I even wrote it for you, and, whether they realized it or not, others said their lines, but you ignored it. You went with your wisdom—with your script, rather than mine."

"Father, I was wrong."

"Well, you're in luck. I'm God, and you're not. I have this amazing ability to turn even the worst catastrophes into awesome, Me-glorifying things, so I want you to continue going until I tell you to stop."

"How will I know?"

"You'll know."

"Okay, got a deal for you. I am selfish and self-centered. I don't even know what I need."

"That's quite apparent, but I'm willing to work with you anyway. What's your deal?"

"I won't ask anybody, except you, for anything. If you want me to have it, you're going to have to give it to me. If you don't want me to have it, don't give it to me."

"Deal. Let me make sure we're clear. I give you what I want to, and you will thankfully receive it? Anything I think is wrong for you, I will withhold, and you'll be thankful for the things I don't give you as well?"

"Yes, Father"

"It's about time. Now, keep walking, Dave."

"Yes, sir."

I walked and walked. Not a soul even seemed to notice my upturned thumb.

One thing I learned early in life was how to hike a challenging trail. My parents always planned two weeks of vacation every summer with the family. The first week was the action week, often in the North Carolina Appalachian Mountains. The yearly intention for the second week was to be a week of rest at Myrtle Beach, South Carolina. "Intention," I say because that week of rest might include a 6 a.m. jog down the beach to a fishing pier, a late-night excursion gigging for flounder or crabs, or riding "Rover" (a durable rubber raft) on the surf to see who could stay in it. However, we learned real durability lessons on hiking and backpacking trails in the North Carolina Appalachians. If you wanted to get back to "civilization," otherwise known as the campground, you had to put one foot in front of the other. There were no choices in the matter. Even if there had been cell phones at the time, there would have been no signals in some of the places we went; you could forget "phone-a-friend" for a quick rescue. There was simply the choice between going nowhere and putting one foot in front of the other, no matter how tired you might be.

So, I walked. The sky cleared. That was cool. A car made a U-turn and pulled over in front of me. That was cooler. A young man rolled down the window and asked me,

"Where are you headed?" That was the coolest.

"As far north as you are," I replied.

"Oh, well, you can hop in, but I am only going to Walmart."

Even though I could look ahead and see the Walmart sign in the distance, I gladly hopped in. I was already tired, and any ride was better than no ride. I told him I appreciated the lift, and I was on a journey of faith, and I was a Christian.

He immediately glowed, "I'm kind of new to this life. I have just become a Christian, and I need to learn more about walking by faith."

At that moment, I felt the overwhelming sense that God was at work in his life, and God had timed my walk with this young man's U-turn. I felt the humbling realization that I was inadequate to the task of positively affecting his life. I was not only financially bankrupt, but spiritually bankrupt as well, or so I thought.

Out of my mouth began to pour some well-placed words of wisdom that impacted him. The import of what I was saying was evident on his face. In the ten minutes I spent with this young man, talking and praying with him in the Walmart parking lot, I discovered something. I may have been spiritually bank-rupt, but I had the keys to my Heavenly Fa-ther's spiritual bank. All I had to do was open the vault and let the wealth pour through me. After all, the spiritual wealth isn't mine—it is God's, and I can access it anytime He calls on me to do so. My spirits rose, and I felt encour-aged. God wasn't done with me yet. I walked out of the Walmart parking lot in Lovejoy, crossed the highway, stuck out my thumb, and it began to rain.

I walked a few more miles. Arriving in southern Jonesboro, just as the rain started to fall in earnest, I glanced across the street, and I saw a church where services were about to commence; people were arriving and turning into the parking lot. Unusual, I thought, since most churches had shifted away from having Sunday night services.

It occurred to me that I could handle a dry place for an hour or so, and after my earlier ex-perience, I felt like a church service would be good right about now.

Even though my parents raised us as Southern Baptists, they had taught me early on that denominations were simply our extended family, and while we may not agree with everything they may teach, we should allow others room to be wrong now and then. Just kidding. In reality, my mother had taught me that there were two levels of theology. One was Jesus, and the other was everything else. In the grand scheme of things, everything else doesn't matter because, in essence, only Jesus matters. Only within a relationship with Jesus does any doctrine gain significance. I walked across the highway to the church, not even bothering to see what denomination it was because it was a dry place.

A gentleman opened the door for me, and took one look at me,

"You want some hot coffee and a towel? My name is T."

"I would love some."

I am, after all, from the South. Though coffee is not my favorite drink, sounding pleasant and appreciative is a necessary part of social communication. That, and I was cold and thankful for the kindness. I had not been shown much kindness in recent months, and I yearned for some kind of positive human interaction. Thinking T was going to pour me a cup of coffee made me feel warm inside already.

Following him into the kitchen, I quickly came to realize I was more special to him than I thought, as he dug out the coffee maker, coffee, filters, sugar, and cream and began the process of finding me a clean towel. He hadn't merely offered me a cup of coffee from some already brewed. He made a pot of coffee, just for me.

Sometimes, I can be obtuse, but God's graciousness, exhibited through the compassion of His servant T, did not escape my notice.

"Are you hungry?" he asked. "I'm sure you are. The church service is about to start. If you want to hang around, see me afterward. I'll hook you up. Make yourself at home." Not wanting to be late, T hurriedly strode to the worship center.

As I sat in the entry area of the church, drying my hair and drinking my coffee, the tears began to flow. My feet already hurt. I was wet and cold. I was miserable, and T told me to make myself at home in God's house. Hard-headed, stubborn, and strong-willed, I still got the message from my Heavenly Father. I was at home in His house.

I finished my coffee and eased into the service. I could not see T. The truth is I really couldn't see anybody. Three months earlier, someone had been so kind as to shatter my glasses into a million pieces—while breaking some bones and giving me a concussion.

I eased into a pew and joined in the service. I love music, and the praise and worship portion continued to bring quiet tears to my eyes.

I discovered the pastor was not speaking that evening. They had a guest speaker who was a missionary to Central America. Now, that may not mean anything to you, but my mother dedicated her last many years to mission work, and while going all over the world, her second language was Spanish. The most significant portion of her work was in Central and South America. "Coincidences are God's way of showing He is in control," reads one of my favorite bumper stickers. It comforted me to hear the speaker's scripture reading in Spanish and his anecdotes from that region of the world.

Within a minute of the final, "Amen," T found me. "You're still here," T declared with pleasure.

T corralled me toward the back of the church. He introduced me to his wife, and they began to find some food in the church's mission pantry. Mrs. T loaded a bag down, and I almost asked about a backpack when T rounded the corner, took one look, and disappeared—only to reappear with a pack and cans with easy-open lids. No requests by me, he simply gave me a U.S. Air Force backpack full of food, food that was completely accessible, with the pull of a ring-tab.

God's grace. It's amazing. Someone should write a song about that.

As I walked out of the Apostolic Tabernacle in Jonesboro, Georgia, with a stocked backpack, sated hunger, and full, yet lighter, spirit, T handed me one last thing, a new umbrella.

Wow! The rain had ceased while the service was going on. Things weren't going gangbusters, but life had a better feel.

The coolest so far!

I walked across the highway and headed north into the now night-darkened sky. At roughly 100 yards north, give or take a few feet, it began to rain again.

"Lord, I already told you I am not gonna curse you and die. Oh, Lord, You're beautiful. Your face is all I seek. For when your eyes are on this child, your Grace abounds to me." I sang. I sang reverently, I might add.

I walked; it rained harder. I prayed; it rained more. As I sang, I began to stumble, and I dropped my worthless hitchhiking thumb.

"Lord. Not tryin' to ask for too much, but nobody seems to see me, and I'm getting tired.

I have walked a long way. I am not stopping 'til you tell me to, but I could use some help here," I said, as exhaustion poured over me.

However, within 30 seconds of my plea, I noticed the sudden brightening of the US 19/41 emergency lane in front of me—my exhausted silhouette outlined by lights.

It was a MARTA city bus. It pulled up beside me, and the door opened. I looked up at the bus driver,

"Ma'am, I only have eighty-three cents to my name." My brother's fifteen was already almost gone.

"Get on this bus, you fool. It's raining," she said with a smile. Relief does not begin to describe my physical, much less emotional response.

God's mercy. Who am I?

He cared enough to send a MARTA bus to arrive at my point of desperation. He cared enough to die, but He cares enough to live for us too. And not just good folks, but losers like me. "Really, Father? Who am I?"

"Well, thank you, Lord. You are an awesome God," I threw up a quick prayer.

I don't know if it was in sheer desperation for the walk to be over, or I thought that my travails were behind me. I mean, in my head, I knew exactly how this was going to play out.

Before leaving Griffin, a friend told me Greyhound would ship me anywhere for free if I said I was homeless.

I was now inside the Atlanta transit system. I had only ridden a MARTA train once or twice and had never been on a bus, but I knew now I could get to Boston or L.A. without a hitch. (I still had no clue where I would end up).

It stopped raining. If it were only daytime, the sun would have been shining bright, and the bluebirds would have been singing, "Zip-a-dee-doo-dah, Zip-a-dee-ay."

The bus deposited me at the subway station, but I had no transfer pass for the train.

"Bump in the road. That's all this is."

I stood there for several minutes. I needed to get on the train. To do that, I needed to get through the turnstiles. To get through the turnstiles, I needed money, a MARTA card, or something. I stared for a few minutes. I started to ask someone, but remembered my promise when up walked a MARTA employee who asked me,

"Do you need to get on the train?"

Looking up, "Wow! God, you are really on point!"

I said, "Yes," was let through the turnstile, and proceeded to wait for the train. I got on, rode a few stops, and got off.

It was all over but the cryin'!

There was the Greyhound bus station. All I had to do was walk in, explain that I was homeless, and they would give me a bus ticket to anywhere but where I was.

WOO-HOOO!

Track 3: Perplexity and Peace

Perplexed = bewildered, confused, and disturbed by it!

I was there. My mind and my spirit were experiencing everything my physical being was going through in a whole other dimension. My previous life was a mess. My current situation was confounding. The people around me, my immediate needs, yes, and the storm itself were punctuating what was occurring inside me.

One cannot be at peace and be perplexed at the same time.

As God dealt with me, I began to have a peace I did not comprehend. As troubles assaulted me, I would find a little more peace infused by the Spirit. Puzzled that He could accomplish peace in my life, no matter the outward circumstances, does not equal perplexed.

The kind of peace He offers goes beyond explanation, yet it provided completeness I had never experienced.

While you may discover the Greyhound employees and the drug dealers within this piece, the most consistent theme of this composition is that out of the dissonance of chaos, the Lord can provide peace.

"I am leaving you with a gift–peace of heart and mind. And the peace I give is a gift the world cannot give, so don't be troubled or afraid."
John 14:27 (NLT)

2
Mixing the Dough

"Sir, I don't believe Greyhound does that anymore, but you can talk to a supervisor," said an attendant. Not a problem. I just needed to turn on the charm and use my God-given, well-trained tongue to my advantage.

"Sir, there are agencies that can help you. We are not one of them. And you need to leave," said the supervisor flatly.

Talk about being shot down! To add insult to injury, as I tried to adjust my backpack straps so that I could leave, a security guy informed me I needed to get out.

Wow! Crash and burn!

I replied to him, "Buddy, I just got out of the hospital. Give me a second."

"If you need an ambulance, go across the street. I'm sure the police over there will help. Now get out!"

There was no mercy here. I walked away, and drug dealers immediately accosted me, offering their wares.

I fled.

I got roughly two blocks, and a flood fell from the sky. I say it like that because this wasn't rain in the ordinary sense. In Texas, they'd call it a "gullywasher." In Georgia, "It's raining cats and dogs." Only if that were true, it'd have been cats the size of tigers and dogs with the size and ferocity of werewolves. In less than thirty seconds, rain permeated everything I had on to the skin. I noticed that water was even sloshing out of the top of my tightly tied work boots. I looked around to see if Noah and his ark were nearby.

Even if I could have seen without my glasses, I could not have seen past the sheet of water flowing earthward. I was breathing water in with every breath, literally choking on it at one point. The wind whipped the umbrella from my hand, then negated its usefulness when I caught up to it.

I managed about three miles in this, trying to go anywhere but the bottom of the water-world, to which I had apparently been tele-ported by aliens disguised as Greyhound security guys.

As I walked, I sang praises and prayed—anything that at least kept the air going out of, rather than water flowing into my mouth.

I was attempting to prove to God that I could at least go through the motions, but I wasn't feeling it. No, really, I promise, before I even had walked a mile, I wasn't feeling anything but pain—then cold—then nothing, as hypothermia began to set in.

As I approached one intersection, the wind and rain came at me from the south. The next, it came from the north—front, back, and ever downward—seeking to grind me into the pave-ment. I do not exaggerate. From a purely ob-jective standpoint, it was an awe-inspiring storm. I have worked in hurricanes that couldn't touch what I experienced that night.

"O Lord, you're beautiful…." One foot in front of the other and occasionally, "Having done all to stand," I simply stood trying not to topple over. I stumbled into a MARTA train station—no longer in operation for the night, but,

"Thank you, Father, for shelter from this maelstrom."

I knew I was in bad shape. I had stopped shivering awhile before—not a favorable medical sign. I curled up on the concrete platform and dozed off.

I awoke with a start. I heard voices around the corner, and I didn't want any trouble with the police. I tried to get up and had to pull myself up with my hands. My legs did not want to cooperate. Not good! I wandered back out into the rain. I had to keep moving.

A hundred feet from the train station, I saw a sign, "Emory," a hospital. I wandered into the emergency room and asked permission to get warm.

"We're not supposed to let you, but you can sit for a few minutes."

It was warm. I began to shiver again, and as if on cue, the E.R. nurse told me that my time was up. 15-20 minutes was all they would give. It was enough for now.

I walked on.

It rained on.

Finally, the sun began to filter through the darkness, and the rain started to ease up. I found a bench on the leeward side of a building. Exhausted, I slept for 15 or 20 minutes while early morning commuters began their rush through wet streets trying to survive one more day in their own personal rat races.

Too soon, I struggled to my feet and resumed my journey.

"Lord. It's that time again. I know that you know, but I have to ask for some relief."

Almost at the point of falling, I raised my eyes as I rounded a curve on the now heavily traveled surface street. The rain stopped immediately. The sun came out. I almost waited for the "Ahhhh" of an angelic choir—for right in front of me, beneath the clearing sky, was a Chick-fil-A.

"Wow! Lord, when you do it, you do it right!" Not only relief but a refuge as well.

For those who are not familiar with the quick service, fast food not in name only, restaurant, Chick-fil-A, I believe it has Christ-centered compassion as a company policy.

I stumbled through the door and asked to speak to the manager.

"I cannot be a customer today, but I desperately need to sit down."

Without a second thought, the manager said, with a caring smile on his face and a gentle tone, "Buddy, you can not only sit down, but you are also welcome to stay as long as you want. Anything you need, just ask me."

"Just a place to sit down, and thank you."

I found a corner, set my backpack down, collapsed on a chair, and immediately went to sleep.

Note to the world: What would most places of business do with a bedraggled back-pack-laden and soaked man? They surely would not allow him to sleep in their business. Chick-fil-A has broken with typical business models. They close on Sundays—one of the most profitable days of the week for a restaurant. They give away food by the tons to needy people. They let bedraggled, backpack-toting men sleep in their place of business—oh yeah—while the backpack leaves a four-foot diameter puddle of water on the floor. Yet, they are one of the most profitable and fastest-growing companies out there. For all you business model designers, I am sure you would not be able to plan for those results without putting God first.

I woke, somewhat embarrassed over both sleeping and the puddle. I approached a young lady, college age, I'm guessing,

"May I get a mop so that I can clean up my mess," I asked sheepishly while pointing at what looked like a miniature model of Skull Island in the dining area.

Without thinking, she responded, "Of course not, sir. You are our guest. I'll clean it up."

Kindness in a given situation speaks volumes about the inner condition of the heart. She was, in my observation, a young woman raised with Jesus first—taught through word and example by her parents and her supervisors at work.

Compassion—it felt so good just to feel it in action. I might be human, after all.

By no means was I fresh, but I felt better. I walked and came upon the Atlanta Cathedral sitting side by side with Second Ponce De Leon Baptist Church.

"Interesting," I thought. I had never been inside the Atlanta Cathedral. I am not Catholic, but I have long admired the construction of Catholic cathedrals and have had the opportunity to visit a few of them.

I walked into the building. It was indeed, beautiful. There is a certain serenity that allows for good meditation in a beautiful, well-built sanctuary, and this one qualified. I saw no one, and I sat for a moment and meditated. I felt at ease. It was a good feeling.

By the way, I have a slight piano dysfunction. I love to play, though I play mostly for myself—even when playing for others. It is a pure, sane, and legal escape. I intentionally seek out pianos when I am in a house, church, mall—pretty much anywhere. I saw no piano. I wandered around for another moment, walked outside, and enjoyed the prayer garden.

One thing I knew for sure. The Baptist church next door would not have one piano; it would have several. I walked next door and walked in.

"May I help you," a voice rang out from somewhere. Finally, I zeroed in on the source, turned to the right, and saw the friendly face that matched the voice.

"I was just next door and enjoyed seeing the Cathedral's sanctuary."

"Well, would you like to see ours?" she asked—as if sanctuary and worship center inspectors showed up every day at her door, blown in from a recent sky-destroying storm and looking road-worn and soaked to the skin.

"Sure!"

"Just go right up those stairs and through the door."

"Thanks."

I walked into the worship center. I might be bold, some would say brash or, at the very least brazen, but I respected the apparent history of the church I was in and did not sit down at the piano. I wasn't even going to ask. Looking down at myself and imagining how I must appear, I could not drum up the confidence to ask. There was no way a sane person who cared about a good instrument would allow me, in my current condition, to sit down at that piano.

As I walked past the office, I yelled a quick thanks and proceeded to the door.

"Sir! Sir! Wouldn't you like to speak to someone?" I heard behind me.

I backtracked to the office door. I answered affirmatively and sat down on a comfortably soft chair. The wait wasn't long.

"Hi, I'm David Hull."

"David Riordan, here. I think I may be able to remember your first name, although these days, I forget my own name sometimes."

He chuckled at my not-so-funny self-deprecation as if he knew exactly what I meant through personal experience. I continue to be amazed at the compassion of some people who acted as if there was nothing unusual about my appearance, or the way I showed up at their door. I liked this guy. I felt comfortable.

"So, what's going on in your life that brings you here?"

Trusting him completely and without hesitation, I launched into the short version of what you will be reading as soon as you get out of this Prelude. He listened attentively—never interrupting—and without openly passing judgment said,

"I don't know how you are going to get to where you are going. I can't do anything for you there, but I can pray with you."

"That'd be great," I replied.

He prayed. I left.

As I walked away, "Come on, Lord. This was a great place, and You could have helped me out. I am exhausted, I need some help, and this church is capable. What's the deal? I do appreciate the prayer and all. Don't get me wrong, but is this guy just out of tune or what?"

I immediately felt the presence of a Fatherly frown.

"Okay, okay, okay, but this was a great opportunity for you to shine."

Frown deepened. "There is certainly nothing wrong with my 'shine' and nothing wrong with what David just did. He, unlike somebody else I know, knows how to follow directions. I have something better ahead."

"I am thankful, Lord, and you noticed, I hope, that I did not ask for anything."

"You get a gold star. There was a multipart agreement if I remember right, and I, unlike somebody else I know, do not forget my agreements. You are supposed to be just as thankful when I say no as when I spoil you with blessings."

"I'm trying."

"No try, just do."

"Father. Come on now. Stealing lines from George Lucas? Really?"

"Silence, David, before you get yourself into a real pickle with Me! I don't steal; I don't have to steal because everything belongs to me anyway. Who do you think gave the genius to George to create Yoda much less, write the lines? I'm not doing 40 chapters of Job with you. Been there, done that, had it written. Go read it!"

"Sorry. I didn't mean 'steal' steal. Just trying to be funny."

"I'm not laughing, and I know what you were trying to do. Don't push it."

"I really am sorry."

"I know. Get past it. I have."

"Thanks."

"Thanks for remembering to say, 'thanks.' Your mother taught you well. Now, you know how to bake bread? Before you have that great house-filling scent and then eat it, the dough has to be kneaded and put in the oven. I am the Baker, and you are the dough. I have not yet completed the kneading process, and you do not yet smell very good—trust Me on that one—though the rain is helping. As you have told many people, 'In order to get through it, you gotta go through it.'"

He continued, "Get back to your journey. I have some kneading to do."

Track 4: Gardener

He goes by many names, and a rose by any other name remains the same. The Potter, the Carpenter, the Fisher of Men, the Good Shepherd, and of course, the Baker—whatever role He needs to play to reach us reveals His true identity, for God is Love.

From the plant being uprooted to the dough being kneaded, change is never comfortable and is often painful. For me to change, something had to pass away, and for me to reach the point of life-altering faith, as some may say, "God had to take me down through there!"

When cooking, sugar is just sugar until it reaches about 236 degrees F. Then something almost magical happens as the sugar molecules realign. It reaches the softball stage, and grainy sugar becomes smooth, creamy fudge.

With the application of heat and a few other ingredients, sugar becomes icing for a cake.

By this point in my story, I was being mixed, and I needed a few more ingredients and the heat. God provided them as only He can.

"Now, if anyone is enfolded into Christ,
he has become an entirely new creation.
All that is related to the old order has
vanished. Behold, everything
is fresh and new."
2 Corinthians 5:17 (TPT)

3
Kneading the Dough

The misery of each step returned, and my feet were getting in worse shape. Wet boots and wet socks were not helping. Around a corner appeared another well-timed blessing—a church. I was bound and determined to keep my word, but I could not take many more steps. Staying in touch with God's people was not breaking that promise of not asking. The door was open. "Thank you, Lord." Through the door, I trudged or shuffled or stumbled; I can't decide what I would call my gait at that point.

"How may I help you?" spoke the receptionist.

Before I could help myself, my tongue, seemingly of its own accord, blurted, "A dry pair of socks would be awesome."

"You idiot," I thought to myself, "There may be no question mark after it, but that is asking, no getting around it." I am one of my worst judges and critics.

"Do you have a picture I.D?"

"Picture I.D.? You gotta be kidding," I thought.

"No, Ma'am."

Before my mind could launch itself into a silent, resentful diatribe, she said, "I think maybe we could help you out with some socks at least, although next time you stop in, you'll have to have a picture I.D. Have a seat and let me see what I can do."

A few minutes later, another woman came through the door carrying a bag in her hand. "Let's see if any of these will work for you."

Oh, my Lord! I don't think I had ever seen such a blessed sight. It was a whole bag of socks—dry socks at that! If you've ever walked on "dish-pan" feet, you know how I felt. She told me to take as many pairs as I needed.

I sat chagrined. "Lord, I pretty much broke my promise, and yet You give me not just what I asked for, but more. You are indeed an awesome God!

"Now, in this bag," as she produced a second one, "is a little food and a MARTA pass so that maybe you can get off your feet for a few minutes while you get to wherever you're going."

There is no word to describe my embarrassment as I stood before my Lord. I simply hung my head.

She said, "It is starting to rain again. You just sit here as long as you need to and stay dry. I'll get you an umbrella."

She gave me a new umbrella to replace the one torn by the wind during the previous night. Then she looked me in the eyes and said,

"We don't do this, but I want you to have this," as she slipped a folded twenty into my hand.

Wow. When would I ever learn that God would take care of me? When would I open my stubborn eyes and see the truth? All I could do was say thanks through choked, heartfelt tears, and head out the door of what I discovered after the fact was Peachtree Road United Methodist Church.

I headed to the nearest bus stop. Riding—not walking—is healing in and of itself. It is also a lot quicker. Before I realized it, I was on a train. Then another bus taking me further north.

While I had not forgotten that our Father still had some kneading to do, once again, I fell into that trap of feeling everything was worked out.

Easy rider.

As the bus went further north into Gwinnett County, I drifted into a conversation with an older man.

I was becoming aware God had placed me in the path of certain people for specific reasons. The first had been the young man in Henry County. Now I was face-to-face with another appointment.

This man began to explain how he had been delving into science to find the meaning of life. What he had been delving into was mysticism in the guise of "intelli-speak." The world has begun to mistake science for whatever some scientist says. One of the great minds of science, who recently passed away, Stephen Hawking, is guilty of helping along with this new-fangled religion. He did not clarify the difference between real science, as determined by the scientific method, and pseudo-science, as determined by whatever passes the lips of a well-thought-of intelligent man.

This older man, with whom I was discussing the meaning of life, had gone down every imaginable philosophical, pseudo-scientific road. I listened as the bus reached its apex and began its trip back south, but I was not about to walk away from a God-timed appointment.

He believed there is a God, but there is no possible way we could know Him. He felt the world in which we live, and out of which we view our existence is entirely determined by our confused minds, thus eliminating our ability to contact the Almighty.

As before, God's wealth of information began to flow through me.

"Fascinating point of view!" I stated. "I pretty much agree with everything you have just said."

You could have pushed him over with a feather.

"I believe that you are right—with a caveat. We have completely lost our ability to contact God through our own doing. We confuse ourselves more and more with every passing day, but I also believe that the answer is a lot simpler than we could realize on our own."

I had his attention now. He was a man on a real search who had finally reached the right conclusion. On our own, we are desperately and hopelessly lost. We can have the brightest minds of our generation seeking the truth and miss it by the entire cosmos.

That lost!

"You see, I, like you, believe there is a God. There has to be. We know the Second Law of Thermodynamics says that everything runs down and cannot be salvaged after a certain point. Entropy rules everything. That being the case, there is a definite end of things."

I had his rapt attention now.

"If there is a definite end, there had to be a beginning to this creation."

He responded, "I don't have a problem with any of that so far."

"Well, it is pretty obvious, and not trying to be simplistic, the answer is simple. If we cannot bridge the gap between our Creator and ourselves, maybe He can." Before he could interrupt, I went on, "If the Creator is so powerful that He could make the intricacy that we can see in cellular structure and the vastness of the cosmos, don't you think He could manage to find a way to communicate with little old us?"

Dumbfounded, the man just stared at me, obviously having never considered that the Almighty might desire talking to us inferior beings.

"In fact," I said, "I would venture that your opinion of the human race is about where it should be. We have misused and abused God's creation. We have spit in His face, but just as any father does, He loves his children anyway. Love, my friend, is what you have left out of your God-equation. I believe He loves us enough that He was willing to become a man and prove it, thus bridging the gaps of communication and knowledge between Him and us."

I continued to explain the answer was easy. It is the simplicity of love with the complexity of God's grace. Much as an uninformed person has no concept as to how to build a road, he can still drive down it. God paved the path with love. We may not understand everything it took to make that path because the reasons are like the sophisticated road construction techniques used to build our roads—beyond our conception until we learn some facts and gain some experience. Despite our lack of knowledge, it does not hamper our travels.

"And if you don't believe me, ask Him. If God is indeed powerful enough to create this complexity, He is powerful enough to answer your questions. All you gotta do is ask Him. He is powerful enough to hear your voice and distinguish your questions from mine. After all, I have questions I ask Him, and He is rather engaged in answering mine right now, but He can handle the load of all of us. He is God."

As we talked, we had reached his stop and had disembarked. He wanted to go home and continue our conversation, but I looked up to discover there was a Chick-fil-A right in front of the bus stop. Somehow, I knew that another timely appointment was awaiting me inside. I told him that he had heard what I had to say. His real answers would come from our Creator. "Go home and ask Him. I am sure He will answer."

Track 5: Walk of Faith

What is faith? And, better yet, what is the walk of faith?

Faith begins and ends with God. It is the sure knowledge God will walk beside us in our journeys. Early on in my walk, I had proclaimed to the young man in Henry County that I was stepping out on faith.

That's what I wanted. It was arguably a crisis of faith. I needed what I did not have.

I had given up on the idea that I could arrive at anything significant for my life. I called out to God.

He had answered.

Substance and evidence build our faith. It was through His answer that I began to gain faith.

God had begun to deal with me several days earlier, first through a Sergeant of the Spalding County Sheriff's Department, and then through my brother.

The beginning of God's call was in a way I could understand—through others.

That initial contact drew me closer to an understanding that I needed to reach out to Him. I saw God at work in and through others. It became a compelling drive to experience God the way they did.

In this piece, God's call starts a process, and the journey commences. There are highs and lows. These are the building blocks of faith. In the beginning, God is enigmatic. We experience Him, get to know Him, and the mystery fades as our faith grows. Then the Spirit speaks again, the mystery reconstitutes, and God calls us down yet more unknown roads.

We may not know what lies down the paths we travel, but in knowing God, we know He goes before us.

Crises averted.

There's the old saying, "seeing is believing," which gives rise to another old expression, "blind belief." Seeing may be believing, but faith is more than seeing. It is more than belief.

Faith is knowing, though it has not happened yet.

Our eyes may be fooled, but God-birthed faith cannot be.

"You see, in the good news, God's restorative justice is revealed. And as we will see, it begins and ends in faith. As the scripture declares, 'By faith, the just will obtain life.'" Romans 1:17 (VOICE)

4
The Dough Rises

Woohoo! I had that twenty, and I could afford to eat at Chick-fil-A this time. I could actually be a customer! I walked to the counter and ordered, sat down at the only empty table in the place, and bit into one of the best chicken sandwiches I had ever eaten.

I thought, "Man! This is good! Those waffle fries will be good in just a moment."

You see, I am what my mother labeled me, a "Lazy-Susan" eater. You know, those large round serving plates that sit in the middle of a table? You can spin them around and take portions of different items for yourself. I eat by turning my plate to the next thing. I don't mix up my foods either. Why spoil one great taste by getting the juice of something else on it, even if that other thing is excellent? Well, while

I was considering a "Lazy-Suzy" eating faux pas, testing a waffle fry before finishing my sandwich, I noticed a smiling face standing beside my table.

Why Sally decided to stop at my table, I have not the foggiest mortal explanation. It was a God thing, for there can be no other conclusion. I was not the only person by themselves at a table, I was not the only one with a backpack, and I wasn't the roughest looking person in the joint. I had been relatively dry for hours now, so I did not look completely unkempt. I may have looked tired, but I don't think I was any more noticeable than anyone else.

It was a God-timed appointment.

"How are you today?" she asked.

"It's been a long day for me," I responded and explained that I was on a journey of faith. We then launched into a conversation about faith and hope. I expounded that real faith and hope are not some 'pie in the sky' flimsy feelings.

"Now faith is the substance of things hoped for, the evidence of things not seen," I quoted from Hebrews 11:1 in the New Testament. "Substance and evidence. It's incredible to me how we have lost our ability to dissect an English sentence. Prepositional phrases modify a specific noun. The nouns, in this case, are substance and evidence, and yet, we seem to get distracted by the 'things hoped for' and 'things not seen.' Those are modifiers and not the point or object. The nouns are substance and evidence, so faith is substance and evidence—not some wispy, limp-handed, 'Gee, I guess it might be sort of possible' kind of feeling. Faith is an absolute, hard-core knowledge that something will happen—even though it has not happened yet. We exercise faith when we step on a concrete sidewalk for the first time. Why? Because we have previously walked on concrete, and it has not failed us. That is faith. I know my Father will take care of me because He has done it over and over. He goes before me in all things. I know this. I have no doubt He will continue because He has never failed me."

Sally just looked at me as I wrapped up my mini sermon.

She said, "Now David, I know you will believe me when I tell you this, but nobody else would. I lead a discipleship group of younger women that meets on Monday nights—here in just a few hours. You come in here on a 'journey of faith' and launch into this conversation about faith and hope. We wrote the curriculum for the discipleship training months ago. We determined the time-frame months ago when we started this group. The topic of tonight's study is 'Faith and Hope.' It is staggering to believe that God cares enough to send you through this door at this time when I needed to hear what you had to say to share it with these young ladies."

I replied, "No. What's staggering is that God would use an individual who everyone has lost hope in to deliver the message you needed to hear—staggering and humbling."

I had to retire to the restroom to blow my nose and dry my eyes.

When I returned to the table, the manager of the restaurant had returned the money I had spent on my meal, and a cashier, I believe, had paid for two more sandwiches to take with me. It was clear Sally had been sharing my story.

I must take a moment and speak about this fantastic restaurant chain again. They break "sound business practices" every day. They give and give. No one complained as Sally stood and then sat at my table to talk to me. No one griped about providing my meal and additional food at company and employee expense. If I had my guess, if the corporate offices of Chick-fil-A found out, the company would praise them for their actions. They would put them on a pedestal of what the company stands for—being Ambassadors for Christ. They are fearless in their stance of compassion for others. I have seen it first-hand, and you will notice that in this time of being kneaded by the Master Baker, they were who God used to give me relief when I sorely needed it. Later, you'll find, God used them yet again.

At this point, Chick-fil-A was God's sanctuary, where one washed-up man delivered a message to a lady who needed to hear that message of faith and hope. God uses people and companies who make themselves available in mighty ways. God—not coincidence. In a state with over 250 Chick-fil-A restaurants—in a metropolitan area of nearly six million people—in a restaurant with, just guessing, fifty to seventy-five employees—at a location at a bus-stop beyond where I intended to get off—God brought together one broken man with one active servant to get a poignant illustration and message across to a group of young women in a course designed months earlier for that specific night. Call that a coincidence if you want. I'll call that God's way of getting a message across.

On this, I need to say no more.

Sally showed back up at my table, said she was leaving, and could do no more for me than a ride to the next exit, if I was interested. Of course, I was. At this point, a woman who had never met this hitch-hiking, homeless man brandished her weapon of personal protection—a plastic knife. We laughed. In reality, we both knew what and Who protected her! She dropped me off, and we said our goodbyes, and I proceeded to try to find a ride.

Not long after Sally dropped me off, I walked to the entrance ramp of I-85. A young man stopped and picked me up.

"I'm only going up one exit," he told me.

"God-appointment" read the neon light, which, in my imagination, lit up the sky.

I hopped in without hesitation.

Things were getting pretty impressive. God could and would use me. It was also emotionally exhausting, considering I was an emotional wreck already.

The young man proceeded, in the next ten minutes, to pour out his story. He was facing a potential twenty-five-year prison sentence on the following day. He had rented the van he was driving to move all his stuff from his apartment. Drugs, friends, and a former employer had led him down a path off which only Christ could pull him. I prayed for him.

Like the older man from the bus, he did not want to part company. I have been there, where any friendly face was better than no face at all. Fear of what might happen in court the next day weighed heavily upon his whole being. He, however, had a time constraint with the van, and I had to keep moving.

Onward and upward. Thumb out—or rather back to ignored thumb out. It was a palpable sensation. I suddenly felt a change because I intrinsically knew I had no impending appointments. It seemed nobody could see me. That is what I felt. I also believe that while I was not technically invisible, God did not want me to be seen. It was back to learning time.

I walked into a Walmart and slept for a few minutes on a bench. I had become so unnoticeable that local cops, Walmart employees, and passersby took no notice of me. I was left to myself. I had an overwhelming sense of being alone. I may as well have been Matt Damon stranded on Mars. I was a million miles from nowhere, all alone, yet still in Metro Atlanta. With a sinking, desperate feeling, I realized that my ride had taken I-985, and while I was still going north, it was a northern path that would not carry me any great distances. I did remember that this exit shared a hotspot destination for a lot of travelers. There was also an off-ramp on I-85 to one of the largest malls in the world. I was not entirely out of the way. All I had to do was walk toward I-85. It couldn't be that far. It probably isn't— if you're in a car, you don't make a wrong turn, and it doesn't resume raining.

Track 6: The Cross

It all comes down to crosses—
His and ours.

My journey had finally brought me to that pivotal moment—the excising of the final part of me, or at least who I thought I was.

The truth is, I never had an identity. I never knew who I was meant to be. My best attempts in life had left me trying to fill the empty holes with cheap substitutes: work, knowledge, drugs, and trying to play the hero.

The latter was a desperate effort to rescue another because I could not save myself.

With all of the success I previously had in life, the truth is I was a failure. When I could not find solace in the pursuit of knowledge and career success, I collapsed into addiction, and when I could no longer pursue that obsession, I had tried to help another, and that ended in a resounding failure that almost cost me my life.

The truth is I had to die, but not in the way that those people had tried to take my life, and not from a heart attack, like the one I had suffered only a few days earlier. No, I had to follow the example set before me by Christ. I had to nail my old life to a cross. Dying is a frightening thought. Knowing there is life on the other side in no way lessens the fear, for I didn't know what it was like to live that way. All I knew was, what I had been doing wasn't working.

"We know that our old self was crucified with Him in order that the body of sin might be brought to nothing so that we would no longer be enslaved to sin. So you must consider yourselves dead to sin and alive to God in Christ Jesus."
Romans 6:6, 11 (ESV)

5
Baking the Bread

At one point—soaking wet feet in unbearable pain—mind beginning to lose a grip on reality from hypothermia—chest, pounding in agony—I collapsed against a guardrail and slumped onto the ground. It was clear, even to my tortured mind, that the mall had just closed as hundreds of cars passed by my nearly unconscious body, lying in the mud. Desperation and fear seized my mind.

"Not yet, Lord. Not here, not now, not alone!"

"Son, I am not done with you. They will not see you. They will not stop. Your dependence must be on Me and Me alone. It is a hard thing you are going through. I know, for I made you, and I know your limits better than you do! If you want to get through this, you've got to go through this. Sound familiar?"

"But Lord, I can't take anymore!" I sobbed in anger and fear.

"I know your breaking point better than you do. I love you, but to use you, I have got to get you to lose you, for 'whoever loses his life for My sake will find it.' It can no longer be about you because it has to be about Me. That is why you are here. Only in finding and living out your purpose will you ever find My peace that passes all understanding. That is where you will find sanity and security in this crazy world that you all are making out of what I created."

"David, I have plans for you. Plans for you to prosper. I don't want you to fail. I need you to be at full strength, which, in reality, is My strength. You are rediscovering that you have the keys to my bank of wisdom—even when you are spiritually bankrupt. You also have the keys to my strength, even when you have none left, and you have anything and everything else I created you for that you could ever need. Stop fighting Me! *I AM* the answer that you crave. You know this. You are my child. When will you let Me be your total fulfillment?"

"Whenever you are ready, get up, make that pack lighter. You don't need everything in it. With every step you take tonight, I'll give you the strength you need—no more and no less. I am telling you upfront because I don't want you to stop. I have another appointment for you. Don't worry. No matter if each step feels like it'll be your last, you'll have what you need to take another—one step at a time. Your appointment is waiting. Now, no questions; just hop up when you're ready to depend totally on Me."

I lay there in pain—not believing what God was telling me. The pain in my chest, inability to breathe, agony of my feet, and agony in my mind held a "death grip" on my attention.

Finally, having no other choice, other than lying in the mud, I began to get my hands under me, having no clue how I was going to stand. When I got my hands beneath me, I found that

I could get a knee up. While I did not see how I could draw another breath, at the end of each breath, I found that I could indeed take another. I was not taking one day at a time; this was taking one second at a time.

I finally managed to stand. I looked the way I had come and saw my backpack in the middle of the sidewalk fifty feet back—my umbrella about fifty feet beyond that (inexplicably not being blown by the wind). Remembering what my Father had told me, I unloaded five or six cans of baked beans and a couple of other items—making a noticeable stack that a potential needy person might be able to find. I found that I could, indeed, put on the backpack.

I began to walk once more into another fomenting torrential downpour. Interesting word, foment. The archaic meaning: "to bathe in warm or medicated lotions." Well, there was nothing that felt warm about the rain, yet I warmed with each step. There was nothing that felt medicating about any drop that fell from the sky that night, and a lot fell. However, I felt bathed in some secret medicine that would ultimately bring healing.

I walked alternatively with the umbrella pointed straight ahead or straight behind because the rain was coming at me horizontally. Cars rode by and splashed water on me. Miles fled beneath my feet until I eventually came to I-85.

Well, I reached a bridge that went over I-85. No exit or entrance ramp here. I walked on, hoping to find a frontage road of sorts, but it was not happening!

A mile or so farther on, I saw cars turning to the left at a light. That had to be it.

"Thank you, Lord."

I turned left and walked into a subdivision with no apparent exit. There was one way in and one way out. I arrived at that conclusion intelligently because I walked to the back of the neighborhood, and there was no way out—no way out legally, that is. I stumbled through the mud of a construction site and into a right-of-way cutting all the way back to I-85.

I grumbled to myself, "Well, the police may stop me for walking on an interstate, if they can see me, but there's little chance of that in this rain."

I climbed over the guardrail and walked. Within one-half mile, I saw a sign, "Hamilton Mill Parkway 1 Mile."

Just when I thought I would mount a celebratory party, an eighteen-wheeler zoomed past me, bathing me from a rainwater-filled puddle. I stepped to the side quickly and found my left leg knee deep in a hole. As I fell forward, my left forearm slammed into something hard, and the result was more pain. I put my usable arm underneath me. I had the strength to get back up.

"Lord, you are amazing. I would have bet my last dollar that I would not be able to make it another step, and yet, ten miles on, injured and blinded by wind and rain, I find it okay to get back up. Thank You for being true to Your word."

"It's My way of showing My love for you. Anything less, and you might have died. If you had stopped, you'd have probably died. You would have certainly stepped back out of My will and My plans for you."

"Died? I would have died?" My mind fearfully latched onto words that would not have bothered me only a day earlier.

"You did not stop, though, and I am not a knower of things that don't happen."

"That actually makes sense."

"I pretty much always make sense. It's not Me—it's you. Without My strength, you are finished. How's that for no choice—or not much of a choice? For the rest of your life, that will be your only choice, My way or no way. I'll be sure to let you know when you start to stray. I can assure you that you will not be given as much latitude as I have given you in the past. I have plans, and you are getting up there. I want you to prosper. I want the world to see what *I AM* can do with a washed-up old drug addict, who is a believer with life-altering faith. I have plans specifically for you. Don't let yourself and Me down anymore."

"I'll do my best, Lord."

"I know you will because any step without Me will be without My strength. You know how it feels now to walk physically through My strength. I have got to get you to transfer the knowledge into spiritual things. Now, I think you have just a little way to go before you get there."

As I stood up a little straighter, I looked down at my arm, which was swelling nicely. No question in my mind, I knew a broken bone when I saw one.

I walked that mile in reasonably good spirits, despite the pain in my arm. I climbed the exit ramp and discovered, to my pleasant surprise, a QT gas station.

I went immediately into the bathroom and worked at removing my boots. The boots provided no trouble. It was the socks that were the problem. The injured "dish-panned" skin of my feet was sticking to my socks. I could not help but cry out in pain as I removed the offending socks. I was glad that it was the middle of the night, and no one else was around.

It took an agonizing fifteen minutes or so of changing my socks before I realized that my left arm no longer hurt.

Before I could even say anything, He simply said, "My Grace is Sufficient, and I will not let too much happen that I don't provide a way of escape even if it's 'on my dime,' so to speak. It's always 'on my dime' anyway. I just want you to recognize where it is coming from."

"Thank you, Lord!"

"That, son, is one way of recognizing from where it comes. Obedience is another."

"What do I do now?"

"Do what comes next, listen for My voice, and watch for My direction."

Walking up to the counter in the QT, I said, "Hi. I am kinda stranded. I have money to eat, but I really need to dry out and stay warm. Do you mind if I hang out for a few?"

The QT employee smiled at me, "Listen, I used to work at a gas station where homeless people hung out all the time. It doesn't bother me any. Just don't do anything sketchy, and you can hang out as long as you want."

The fact that he had just labeled me as a homeless person was a "bolt-of-lightning" moment for me. It hurts the first time.

"Thanks," I said, as I got myself a cup of coffee.

Two appointments took place that night. One was a gentleman who had warrants for his arrest. He was tired of running. He was about to call the cops on himself. He decided to hang out for a while also. We talked about the difference Christ could make in his life.

The second was a nurse named John, and he wanted to pray for me. He took the time to do that very thing.

Being admittedly homeless, I did the homeless thing—got two large trash bags and slept in their cover from the rain behind the QT.

Two hours later, I crawled out of my trash bags and walked back around front. The young man with warrants was gone, and it was time for me to leave as well. The manager had arrived for the morning.

I left, heading straight down the street to where the QT clerk had told me there was a rather large church.

"Do what comes next and listen, huh? Lord, I am doing what comes next. And, it is true you indeed keep giving me the strength I cannot in any way claim as my own..."

"Laaaaaadies and gentlemen! Let me direct your attention to the center ring. The Amazing Idiot is there for your viewing pleasure. Watch him as God blesses him with a certifiable string of miracles and see him complain."

Well, for your information, it never got that far because it expended too much energy to complain, and I was beginning to understand. All He wanted me to do was think about right now. I had no choice. Starting to sound familiar? It is a shame to be as certifiably intelligent and unbelievably stupid as I am.

I was living on the edge—not within the margins of the past year—but on the precipice of now. Choose life or death. With Him = life and life more abundantly. Without Him = death for me, or something I am coming to understand as much worse.

I shoved the complaints back down my throat, "O Lord, you're beautiful. Your face is all I seek," I sang and then said, "Lord, I am sorry I keep singing the same song. It just reminds me to seek you."

"Sorry? Look, son, I am the one who created creatures who sing 'Holy, Holy, Holy,' day and night for eternity. You have to understand that those words you sing change every time you repeat them. You are growing, and with each growth spurt, I hear praise that is new and more profound. What may sound like monotony to you is an endlessly changing blessing of praise to Me.

"You hear with your ears, which is one of the ways you only 'know in part,' for one day, you'll know things even as I do. When you sing your simple melodies, I hear a symphony of spiritual quality that continually changes as you grow. There is so much more to this creation than you all will ever discover. It brings glory and honor to Me, but I made it for you. That's how special you are to Me."

"Thanks, Lord. You are awesome. Now, where is that church? That dude said it was only half a mile down this road. I've walked more than that."

"Keep walking."

I walked. I came to a red light at the end of a community park. A man pulled up. I walked toward his open window to ask where this church was. He hurriedly rolled his window up and looked in the other direction. He raced off when the light changed.

Disconcerted, I walked towards another vehicle stopping at the light across the street. You would have thought I was the pilot of a 747, and she was air traffic control without the flashlights. Back and forth from capital X to Y as she motioned me away.

"All I needed were directions. A little kindness and compassion would go a long way!" I shouted at the top of my lungs. I am sure she heard me, as did the drivers in the three cars behind her.

I heard, "Your anger is justified if not inexpertly displayed."

"I hear you, Lord. What would you have me do—sit down and weave a whip and turn over some tables?"

"Now, son, that worked for Me, but it probably wouldn't do you much good in this situation. I'll choose to ignore your sarcasm. One of these days, you are going to learn to appreciate Me. My advice, though not command, is to use the anger to solve something other than simply venting."

"I am listening."

"Now, keep walking."

I did walk, but in the direction from which I came. I had passed a store roughly a quarter mile back. I decided to ask directions, and my Father did not stop me.

"Yeah, buddy, the church you're looking for is just past that light."

Of course, just past the light where I had already been.

I arrived at an empty parking lot. It was only about 7:00 a.m. I sat down in a little café style area the church had out front and dozed.

I awoke. Still nobody.

I walked next door to the animal hospital I had passed on my way into the parking lot.

"Do y'all know anything about this church next door?" I asked the receptionist.

"Not really," the receptionist replied, "I see people in the parking lot from time to time. A lot of them on Sundays."

I walked past the church and looked down the hill at a graveyard.

Feeling full of myself, I quipped, "Well Lord, I found the church. They're all here," as I saw a sign that read "Church Members Only." Coming to a sign that read "Open on Sundays," I wrote a note that asked, "What about Monday-Saturday?" I left it on the sign.

"That, at least, is closer to getting some kind of result. Come on, Dave, don't stir up strife if you are not going to be here to help make a change."

I walked back up the hill, feeling quite the comedian. I dozed off again. Waking, now thoroughly frustrated, I noticed a slew of cars parked behind the animal hospital. I no longer felt like a comedian. Now I felt like a fool.

OMG! The church's offices must be up there, where I could not see them. Behind the hospital, I walked. No offices. Nothing but parked cars with the former occupants now immersed in their morning workouts in the health club beside the animal hospital.

Tired, frustrated, and quite honestly not sure what to do, I walked into the health club.

"May I help you?" came the compassionate and concerned inquiry from the lady at the desk.

"Do you know anything about the church next door?"

"Not much. But, you need some assistance," she stated the obvious.

Without batting an eyelash, or looking down her nose at me, the receptionist picked up the phone and dialed.

As I sat down near the counter on a rather comfortable lobby chair, I went into a brief explanation of what I had been going through. I explained my necessity to get out of town. When asked where I was going, the only possibility that sprung to my lips was Boston—although, the fact was I had toyed with a dozen different locations.

Boston? I thought of Boston because I knew someone there. A few years before, I had worked in the Boston area. While there, I had helped out a young woman who later contacted me on Facebook. We remained online friends. Boston was the only distant place where I knew anybody else. Danielle would at least take my call if I wanted to go there, but that didn't matter. I had just declared Boston as my destination because I couldn't think of anywhere else to go.

Within a few minutes, kind people surrounded me. One gentleman went to his locker and retrieved dry socks and shoes. A few minutes later, a hot, you guessed it, Chick-fil-A meal came through the door.

As I was about to get up, yet a third person walked up and asked, "Didn't you say you were going to Boston?"

"Yes," I replied.

"Good! A friend of mine is buying you a bus ticket."

I was dumbfounded. Several people who had never seen me before—one who still had not even met me—had all miraculously reached out and helped me.

"Miraculous?" you ask. Yes. Fifteen minutes either way, and I would have missed the confluence of individuals that day. God is always on time. After being vetted by some very professional local policemen who treated me with the utmost respect and added nothing but kindness to the equation of the day, I realized the kneading and baking were over, for now. I felt like a warm loaf of bread.

"Lord. Thank you! You could have told me this appointment was for me!"

"Why do that and spoil all the fun? Go ahead. Call Me the Drama King if you like, but

I do like showing off. I created you guys in a way that appreciates the extra effort involved in putting on a production. You are, after all, in My image. I want you to understand how precious you are to Me. Without the kneading and baking processes, how could you truly understand how cool it is when I step into the picture? Plus, bread just doesn't turn out right without being kneaded, and the bread does not get to determine when it is ready. Bread doesn't understand what it needs, nor does it understand the heat of the oven. You have to agree, though, how good it smells when it is baked right by the baker. You, son, are a masterpiece. I am your Baker. You are an awesome sweet-smelling piece of work! That is spiritually speaking. You still need a shower, but everything in its time."

I sang,

"Oh, Lord, you're beautiful.
Your face is all I seek,
for when your eyes are on this child,
Your grace abounds to me.
I want to take Your word
and shine it all around,

but first help me to just live it, Lord.
And when I'm doing well,
help me to never seek a crown,
for my reward is giving glory to You.
Oh, Lord, please light the fire
that once burned bright and clear.
Replace the lamp of my first love
that burns with holy fear."

He responded, "Now, that's a song from those lips worth hearing. It gets better each time! Now, you have a trip to take and some things to do for Me. You're not exactly where I want you yet. You still have some growing to do. I have some incredibly amazing things to show you. I have some healing to give you, and if you think the arm was something, wait till you see what I can do with your heart and mind—if you'll let Me!"

6
Out of the Oven

Having just been issued a nursely command to lie down, I took stock of my situation. This hospital, 90 % closed, had been converted into an emergency-services-only facility by the state of Massachusetts. With its dark windows, viewed as I approached the building, it accentuated my feelings of loneliness—an absolute and conclusive separation from everything that had gone before.

Whatever might come, I did not know. Sheer exhaustion weighed heavily upon me. I was a stumbling bedraggled mess, my legs barely able to communicate the oversized entry —made so to accommodate the injured of the world.

Those two days in the storm had been an incredible time with God. The past two had been equally fulfilling, but I was way beyond— beyond any point I'd ever been physically, emotionally, and certainly spiritually. It was as if the first two days had been an introduction to a new kind of life. The second two had been more of a realization of what it all meant. This realization didn't change my current mess, nor did it imply I was suddenly a greater super-Christian. I was broken, but at least I recognized it, and, more importantly, now I knew in Whose strength I needed to remain.

It had also been a journey deep into unrequited and continued exhaustion. The profundity of my spiritual position was evident; however, so was the reality of my physical situation. Whether I would ever make it back to Georgia, I didn't know. I needed clearness of thought to evaluate everything better, and in my current state, the only thing clear was that I was where I needed to be—in a hospital.

As I lay in the hospital bed, I began to ruminate over all I'd been through, equally questioning both my spiritual and physical destinations.

Track 7: Hymn of Praise to the God Who Changes Hearts

"Agnus Dei," this song begins.

Is He not the Servant of servants?

"Behold the Lamb of God that taketh away the sin of the world," proclaimed John the Baptist.

Indeed, our Lord serves us and motivates us to help others. In my journey, there are two recurring themes. There are the God-appointments, where God sent me to an individual for a specific purpose. However, my brother loves me, and what he noticed were the moments God sent others to minister to me in my time of crisis.

In this journey of faith, God was working some things out in my life, but the call to serve others never dimmed. It is the same for others who have also been called out and set apart. Just as God had begun changing my heart, God had changed others before me. They were answering His call.

He is a God who makes all things new, and this Hymn is to honor Him for all the hearts He has turned towards me!

"A new heart also will I give you, and a new spirit will I put within you: and I will take away the stony heart out of your flesh, and I will give you a heart of flesh."
Ezekiel 36:26 (KJV)

Two days earlier:

I was supposed to have left the Greyhound bus depot near Gainesville, GA, at about 1:00 p.m. heading northward. The roofing contractor who had purchased the ticket for me at the Gwinnett County health club had also secured for me an Uber ride. I arrived about an hour early.

The Uber driver turned out to be another "God Appointment" arranged just for me. As I write this nearly two years later, I had to pull out my notes scribbled on torn paper to remember her name. I may not have remembered Katherine's name, but I remember her impact on me.

An immigrant from a Caribbean island, she was standing on a firm foundation of her faith. I could have gotten any Uber driver, but I got one that fed me Godly encouragement for the forty-five-minute drive to the depot. The feeding was not only spiritual.

"You must be hungry," Katherine said.

"I won't deny it," I admitted, somewhat embarrassed.

"Come with me!" She boldly commanded as she headed towards the door of the convenience store, doubling as a bus depot.

"Now, get what you want!"

Without question, anyone who knows me knows what I did. I headed straight to the back of the store and grabbed a cold Diet Coke and returned to the front counter where Katherine awaited me.

"No, no, no, no!" as she grabbed me, gently forcing me back into the depths of the store. "I said, 'Get something!'"

Reluctantly, but gladly, I grabbed a Three Musketeers. She just shook her head and marched through the store, grabbing a sandwich, chips, a two-liter of Diet Coke, putting the small bag of chips back, and grabbing a larger one. $9.35 later, she was hugging me goodbye, leaving me with a five-dollar bill in my hands. "I'll be praying for you."

I would love to call Katherine an angel. She was undoubtedly my angel, but I don't want to take anything away from the woman. An angel certainly could have been sent to minister to me. They are at God's beck and call. No, she was not an angel.

Katherine was a great example to me of how the Body of Christ should operate. Something cemented itself in me that day by God through Katherine that I continue to use as a guiding principle. In truth, we do not live in the past, nor do we live in the future. We live in the now, and God brings us opportunities to reach others at *His* pace, not ours. If we are focused on the past or future, we will miss those whom God places in our paths.

Waving out the car window and smiling broadly, Katherine hung a right out of the parking lot, leaving me with the bag full of food. I would be glad later I had it to put with my backpack supplies. Variety is a good thing, however, that two liter? It would be gone before the bus pulled away from my current perch.

It would be nine-and-a-half hours of waiting.

Meandering around the parking lot got old fast. I tried to strike up a conversation a time or two. I took a nap on the walkway alongside the building. Bored to tears, I even cleaned the entire parking lot and surrounding grassy areas of trash and took another nap. I checked with the folks inside.

"Delay, delay, and delay," was all they told me.

I walked to the next parking lot, so I could sit and write some notes for a minute in the Waffle House. I stayed there until the restaurant filled with sheriff's deputies. Okay, maybe not "filled," per se, but two tables' worth and a couple at the bar. Too many for my comfort level. I was not yet out of Georgia. They did not make me feel safer. I nodded at the water-glass filling waitress and slipped back out, heading back from whence I came.

And that was just the first hour!

Not really.

By this point, it was 7:30 p.m., and we finally had an ETA from Greyhound. The station owner proclaimed at my query,

"Your bus will be pulling in shortly. It should be here in the next thirty minutes."

I was not unhappy. The past two days may have been an incredible journey, for God had met me where I was. He had spoken with me, touched me, and healed me. He had altered forever how I would walk with Him, but my journey in this life was far from over. Things like waiting on a Greyhound bus still had to take place. I was bone-weary. My body screamed at me, and I cannot begin to express how happy my feet were in new socks and shoes.

Returning to the side walkway, I scrambled around, gathering up socks I had laid out to dry. The sidewalk had looked like a Christmas decoration littered with pink, green, and white socks drying in the early evening air. (By the way, I still have those pink and green furry socks. They are mementos of my time with God and of the kindness of others). I tied my still-wet boots to my backpack. I took the last swig from my Diet Coke, slung my pack on my back, adjusted my cap, and gazed expectantly toward the entry of the lot.

No matter how intently I looked at the entry, that bus just wouldn't pull in. Shucking my backpack, it resumed its waitful stance beside me on the ground.

Grabbing a fresh cold Diet Coke from inside the store, I committed to not open it 'til after I was on the bus. There are just some commitments a man should never make! Slouching onto a bench, I turned back on my "waiting mode."

9:30 pm: Light splashed excitedly across my visual cortex as extreme fatigue had seemingly even thinned the separation between the world and my brain. No matter the narrowing effect of the exhausted tunnel vision I was developing, there was no force I knew that could or would stop me from seeing and boarding that bus—including that very exhaustion. The bus driver opened the door. I climbed aboard, found a seat, and waited patiently to see the "Welcome to South Carolina" sign.

I never saw it! From all I witnessed, they don't put up those signs on backcountry border crossings. This bus made every podunk town stop it could find! I was only 30 minutes from the border, but it took 3 ½ hours before I heard the bus driver declare a specific stop— Something-Or-Another, South Carolina!

Passengers boarded, and passengers disembarked. I changed buses a couple of times. Minutes rolled into more minutes, and hours blurred into more hours. Darkness morphed into dawn, and before I realized it, night filled the bus again as I crossed into New Jersey.

"Ladies and Gentlemen, we are approaching New York City. If you have a connection going to Boston, your route has been canceled due to a maintenance issue with that bus. There will be another bus leaving New York City for Boston at 6:30 in the morning."

Noooooo! Wow, I didn't think I could handle it, but then again, did I have a choice?

As I exited the bus inside the Port Authority Bus Terminal, I saw an LED display above the next bus dock. "Boston." I had an idea. The girl next to me seemed to get it at the same time. I grabbed one of her suitcases, and we made a mad dash to the ticket counter.

Three people back in line. Then just the girl and me. I let her go to the counter first, and almost immediately, the next attendant called me. The girl's attendant stepped away from the desk. Mine said,

"We just had two cancellations for that route, and we can swap out your ticket."

The girl was getting hers at the same time. Behind us was an ever-lengthening line consisting of our previous fellow riders. They had seen the LED sign moments too late. Sadly, they were not to be as fortunate as the girl and me.

Having an hour to burn, I spent it seeing the all-too-bright New York City lights around the station. Upon returning to the bus line, I discovered my bus had arrived, and it was loading. Once again, I was last in line. I allowed the girl to go in front of me. As I boarded behind her, she made for the only available seat near the rear of the bus!

My whole inner being sank into a puddle beneath my feet. I think my heart may have even stopped for a second. I couldn't believe it. I had now been officially on the road since Sunday afternoon—seventy-eight hours! I left Georgia a wreck. I had not recouped in any way. If anything, I was worse off. It took everything I had to face the fact and turn around. It might be nine more hours before I could leave the Big Apple. The realization hit me like a wrecking ball to my soul.

Usually, I would have taken it in stride. I'd never spent more than a few hours in the City, and that had been in the daylight. I was not in good shape, and I was not in the right frame of mind. It didn't matter how bright the lights were; crushed, my spirit seemed to drift into a dark place.

I turned, heartbroken, to head back out of the bus with the realization I'd be in New York City for several more hours. Let's face it. I didn't have anywhere to go when I got to Boston. I'd talked to my friend, Danielle, on a borrowed phone while I was passing through Delaware. Staying with her was not an option. That didn't matter at this point. I just wanted the journey to be over.

As if by magic, the very front row had one available seat. I'd swear it hadn't been there when I got on, but it sure was now! The relief was palpable. It was indescribable. It was awesome!! My seatmate moved his jacket, clearing the way for me to plop down. After twenty-four hours on a bus, who'd think I would be this relieved? You just don't know.

"Hi. My name is Ahmed."

And with that, weariness drained away. My whole being invigorated, pain disappeared, my mind cleared, and my heart said, "God Appointment!"

Ahmed had grown up in the ghetto of the Bronx. Life had not been kind to him. He'd begun running drugs while still in elementary school. He hadn't finished high school before he had graduated to prison. It is an all-too-common story repeated over and over in the inner-city, gang-controlled ghettos.

"But I did everything right after that," he continued to tell me. "I got my GED in prison, and when I got out, I stayed away from the old gang. I stayed away from drugs. I didn't even drink! I got me a real job, met my girl, had a baby, and got married. I love my daughter. She means everything to me, but things went bad with my wife."

And now, we had arrived at the crux of the problem. Now, I saw why Ahmed was on a Greyhound headed to Connecticut.

"It got bad. I couldn't make enough money, and of all people, my girl wanted me to get back involved with my old gang. The money's just too good. I swore I'd never go back, and when I told her I wouldn't, she kicked me out of the apartment and moved some chump in."

Ouch! I could see the pain in his eyes as the light from the road bounced off of them like flashing emergency lights from a frantic ambulance pinned in by rush-hour traffic. Real desperation gripped him, pouring out unrelenting from his soul. I felt it as it washed out of him and over me. No matter how much he let out, it would only regenerate from within his broken heart in a never-ending stream of regret.

"It's not fair. What could I have done differently? I could not go back, but I don't know if I can go on! And now? Now she won't even let me see my daughter."

He continued, "I bought this ticket because if I stayed, I'd only end up back in trouble!"

Ahmed's sister had managed to get out of the inner-city life. She had moved to Hartford, and she had a spare room. She was an oasis. He was desperate and looking for answers. He, at least, had somewhere to land.

He had a brush with Islam in prison. His mom had been a regular at the church he'd stopped attending as a child. He had heard of a dozen different religions, but he didn't know which way to turn nor what to believe. He knew there was a God, for the world was just too beautiful a place.

Ahmed talked for over an hour. I didn't interrupt. I didn't really know what to say, but I intrinsically knew he needed to let it out. When he finished, words began to flow.

Gently, I said, "If what you say is true, and you know there's a God because of everything you see, and if He's powerful enough to create everything, don'tcha think He's powerful enough to talk with you?"

"But why would He?"

Ah, now I understood. Battered and bruised throughout his life, with recent injury punctuating his feelings of hopelessness, Ahmed didn't think he was worthy.

"Ahmed, I understand. You feel hopeless because you've screwed up in life, and you think you're not worth loving. Brother, no matter how people may make you feel, don't confuse that with God. He created you. He loved you enough to become a man and give up His life for you. Not only that, He rose again, so you don't have to live like this. It's not that problems all disappear. It's that He'll walk with you through them all, and what may seem unbearable now will become victories in your life."

"How do I know that's true? How do I know your Jesus is the answer?"

"That's the easy part. I'm not going to sit here and beat you into submission until you believe. It is a rather simple thing and something of which I don't have to convince you. You know there's a God. It makes sense that He can hear you. Talk to Him. He's perfectly able to deal with you in a way you can understand! Jesus made the way possible. Talk to God. He'll do the convincing. He will make Himself real to you."

Ahmed disembarked in Hartford, Connecticut.

I rolled into Boston at three in the morning. Nothing but stone benches awaited me for a place to rest my body, but it was enough. I crashed and burned—that is, until the station came alive at about 5:00 a.m. with the morning commuter traffic.

Hopelessly roused, I wandered down the stairs and out onto the sidewalk. I have to admit I was a bit overwhelmed. It seemed ages since my brother had handed me his last fifteen dollars, but it had only been four days.

"Lord? What am I supposed to do now?"

Downtown Boston is as intimidating as any large unfamiliar city. I felt incredibly alone, but I felt safe for the first time in nearly a year. My disenfranchisement was almost complete with anyone in Georgia; however, I was in the middle of eight million people, and surely, I could make new friends. New friends? I didn't have old friends.

"If I'm gonna get through this, I gotta go through this."

"That's better," I suddenly heard. "Son, why do you think I brought you through all of this?"

"It's obvious you love me," was my unsure response. What was He trying to get out of me?

"Not that My love is that small of a thing, but seriously Dave, do you think it's just all warm fuzzy love? Do you think I'm that single-faceted?"

"No. Not at all. I just don't know what to do. I'm way up here. I know one person within 1000 miles. I'm exhausted like you wouldn't believe!"

"Really? Technically, you are correct. It is not a matter of belief. Dave, I KNOW exactly how tired you are. Do you need a reminder of how I got you through that last night of the storm? I know exactly what you need and exactly where you are."

"Father, I remember. I will never forget."

"I know you won't. I know you, but better than that, *I Am* Me, after all. I don't fail—ever. I created you, and *I Am* making you into who I want you to be. Now you agreed. You need to trust me. I've got this all worked out. I can assure you, it will rarely be the way you think it should be. Let's face it. You don't exactly have the best track record when doing things on your own. At times you'll feel things are impossible, but it will always be for your best and the best of those around you."

"That sounds all fine and well, but what am I supposed to do now?"

"Dave, live your life! Get through every day. Look for the next thing to do with great expectations! I have a lot of things in store for you. If you do as I ask, you'll never truly want for anything. People will most certainly try to harm you. It comes with the territory, so stand firm in this relationship with Me. I'll always provide for you and show you a way to get out if things turn against you. How's that for a commitment from Me?"

"It sounds great. How many people can say they've got you at their back?!"

I felt that displeased look.

"All of my children. Whether they understand it or not, I'm always there."

"Oh yeah. Sorry. I forget who I'm talking to sometimes."

"Dave, it's okay. Just don't ever forget, you are incredibly special to Me, but so are the people you'll find in your path as you go on from here. Love them because I have loved you. Forgive them because I've forgiven you. Carry their burdens with them. Pray for them, and Dave, give because you will always have what you need no matter how much you give."

"How can I say 'no,' to you? Never mind, don't answer that!" I sincerely heard a chuckle!

"See? You are teachable, after all! True, I had to do the whole storm thing, but you can indeed learn—hardheaded, stubborn and indifferent at ..."

"Stop! I get it."

"Oh, I know, heh-heh-heh," He chuckled, "Just having some fun with you. You really should lighten up some. Learn to enjoy what I've given you. Otherwise? Otherwise, you're wasting my efforts. Now, I'm just going to let that lay there. Feel free to pick it up when you're ready."

He paused briefly and continued, "'What do you do?' I believe it is the question of the moment. Live, love, and serve. Walk forward. Live in the moment. Take what I give you and put your best effort into it. I love to see your improvement. It's that whole journey thing again. Let me know when you need Me. I'll be right here beside you anyhow."

"Lord? I Nee..."

Interrupting, "Yes? I know. You need Me. I do have a sense of humor, you know, and I can appreciate your effort, but I do know what you planned to do. It's kind of impossible to play a joke on Me."

I just smiled, knowing that He knew that I knew that He....Well, never mind.

The sun had risen now on the bustling downtown Boston early morning scene, and I was struggling. Fatigue tinged with the discomfort and fear of unfamiliar territory brought back unbidden complaints.

Somewhere between genuine tears and childish whining, I mumbled half to myself and half to God,

"'Seize the moment,' He says. 'Find the joy!' Yeah right. And I know you hear me. I'm just about out of steam! And I know you know that too!"

I shuffled miserably down the sidewalk, looked up, and lo and behold, there was a McDonald's inside the other end of the bus station/commuter rail station in downtown Boston. I could get large Diet Coke and a sausage biscuit for a dollar apiece! I had just enough left over!

Uh, that'd be a resounding "NO!"

Well, Toto, we're not in Georgia anymore! It was my first shot of culture shock. Two dollars and sixty-nine cents later, I had a Diet Coke, no sausage, no biscuit, just one lonely Diet Coke. And, there would be no free refills, I discovered after quickly draining the cup! Ouch!

I didn't want to call Danielle too early, so I waited. So, beginning at 8:00 a.m., I began borrowing phones. I called every fifteen minutes.

No answer.

7
Cooling the Bread

"Well, you've gotten yourself into a mess." Grumbling and moaning, I walked around looking for a new person to accost to try Danielle again. 8:15, 8:30, 8:45, 9:00. Arghhh. How much more? What am I going to do? Despondent, I crumpled to the floor. Leaning back against a wall, I put my head in my hands.

I heard the sound of a throat clearing, "What now, Lord? Can't you see I'm trying to be miserable?"

"What was that, sir?"

Looking up, I realized a familiar man was standing in front of me. I'd used his phone earlier.

"Did you ever get hold of your friend?"

In complete embarrassment, I sputtered, "No. She still hasn't picked up."

Oh, I wasn't embarrassed that he heard me talking to God. I was embarrassed that he heard me talking to God the way I did! He hadn't seemed to notice.

He said, "I'm about to catch an Uber. Before I get out of here, would you like to use my phone again?"

I tried, she answered, and now, I was really embarrassed before God. Once again, my Father had sent me aid when I needed it at the right time. Once again, I was an idiot. I had every reason to trust God, and there I was grumbling and moaning. It must be a long journey to get to the point of not groaning and moaning. I still haven't gotten there despite all of His intervention in my life.

And, you don't know but a fraction of it so far!

I wish you could write accents. If there is a classic "Southie" accent, Danielle has it! Look up "Southie" in the dictionary. Her picture is probably there.

"Now Dave, you're going to have to give me a few minutes. I got to get myself together. It's going to take me an hour and a half to get there on my scoota." Or something to that effect.

Danielle is my buddy. She's a real friend. It would only be after she arrived that I would discover she was extremely ill at the moment.

"Danielle, I hate for you to have to come so far."

"It's okay, Dave. I don't have much, but I've got a phone for you. It's just an Obama phone, but you can't do anything without a phone. You're going to need a phone. I got to bring it to you anyway. Can you get on the Red Line right there in the station and ride it all the way to the end to Braintree?"

"Sure." I had no idea how I was going to ride the subway. I'd just spent my last dime.

It wasn't hard to find the subway entrance. The gate beside the turnstiles was open, and people were flowing through it.

"Thanks, Lord, you are amazing!"

I felt the glow of approval as I headed down the stairs. I boarded the Red Line for what would be the first of hundreds of times before my relationship with the Red Line and my time in Massachusetts would end.

Struggling to keep my eyes open, I waited for Danielle's arrival. Was it a coincidence the Motel 6, where I was working when I originally met Danielle, was on the far side of the subway station complex? With the sputtering sound of a scooter cascading through the air, I thanked God the wait had not been too long.

"Now Dave, I brought'cha this phone. You can't do anything without a phone. And here's a Little Debbie. I don't have any money else I'd give you some," she said with a welcome Southie accent.

It was good to see a familiar face. It was good to feel like somebody cared. I couldn't shake the feeling of being an ant in the middle of a shopping mall. I was tired. I was humanly alone. Boston was a new, enormous place with lots of concrete, asphalt, and buildings. Bostonian accents and culture surrounded me at every turn.

However, Danielle, even with that funky accent, was a sight for sore eyes, and these sore eyes could tell she was ill.

"Danielle, I didn't care if you gave me anything. I'm just glad to see you. I wish you'd told me you were sick! I would never have asked you to come to see me."

"Now Dave, I had to get you this phone, and you need some direction. You're my friend. I couldn't leave you hanging. So, let's start with where you need to go. I have a plan. Dave, you got to get plugged in. You need help."

With that, Danielle plunged into her plan. I needed to go to the hospital and tell them I was suicidal. She told me they'd keep me for a few days, but that would get me into the system, and I'd be able to get the help I needed.

First off, there was no way I was ever going to tell anybody I wanted to kill myself. I might have been in rough shape. I might have been despondent a few days prior, but there was no way I could get those words out of my mouth—not with the way God had rescued me.

Secondly, this just reeked of scam. I'm not one to scam the government. The government didn't have any money. Its money came out of people's pockets. My pride just wasn't going to let me participate.

"Live in the moment," He said. "Take what I give you," He said. There's no way lying to a hospital was what God wanted me to do. There was also no question Danielle was a Godsend. I needed help. I needed some prescriptions; so, the idea was not wholly off-kilter. Where was the balance?

I thanked Danielle profusely. What an act of kindness. What an incredible display of friendship! Danielle prayed for me. We prayed together. We ate our Little Debbies, and then I hurried her off. I had a decision to make, and I wasn't going to be vertical much longer. I finally settled on going to the hospital. It couldn't hurt.

Having seen Danielle off, I asked for directions and headed the couple of miles to the closest hospital.

I panicked as I neared. I could see the parking lot. It was empty, and there were visible signs of idleness. It didn't necessarily look unkempt, and I should know what that looked like. All I had to do was look in the mirror.

I wasn't going to make it to the next hospital. That was a given. There was nothing to do but round the building and check. Giving up seemed to be my only foreseeable option.

The first side, empty. The second side was bereft of people. To the point of shuffling, I turned the corner, and there was an ambulance! Thank God, at least they could transport me to a hospital where there were people!

Someone walked out of the door. I stumbled as I entered, and there was a nurse at the desk.

Track 8: Rest

The title says it all.
Sometimes, you have to rest.

There is so much more to rest than simply lying in a hospital bed. I was certainly in need of physical rest.

The mind and spirit also require a time-out.

I had been running for my life, and I was suffering before the walk began. I'm pretty stubborn and hardheaded, though. It is quite a statement that God would take me through a storm to rearrange my faith, my desires, and my life. It is a statement about the condition of my heart. It also says much about how far God will go for an errant soul.

He is called the Good Shepherd for a reason.

I needed rest, and I got it. I would need more. I would spend many months in rehab for my hand, counseling sessions, and in the Dentist chair, having 24 broken teeth dug out of infected gums. I had a road ahead I still had to travel, but I would go down that road with a different frame of mind and spirit. I had discovered the best kind of rest—resting in Christ.

"Whoever dwells in the shelter of the Most High will rest in the shadow of the Almighty. I will say of the LORD, 'He is my refuge and my fortress.'"
Psalm 91:1, 2 (NIV)

"Sir, you need some help," again, not so much of a question. More of a declaration, much the same as the lady at the health club a thousand miles away now and seemingly years ago.

"I need help," was about all I could squeeze out.

"Come sit down!" she said, escorting me to a chair with a worried look on her face.

Determined to get some help, and equally determined not to lie to do it, I said, "I've been struggling." My mind bent more to the physical. She interpreted psychologically.

"No worries. Come with me," and the nurse led me to a blessed bed.

Whatever worries I had about my ability to acquire help would disappear in the clanging alarms of an automated blood-pressure machine!

Being in the right place, the hospital, was a good thing. Lying down on a real bed, after all I had been through, allowed me to think. God had met me where I was in a pretty fantastic way. He had never left me and returning to Him was relatively simple; a broken heart, a prayer and a song worked.

The only thing that had complicated matters was me, my stubbornness, and my sin. I needed time to soak it all in.

I was about to get some of that commodity.

"Let's check your vitals!"

My reverie was interrupted by a triage nurse in the small partially unused hospital in Quincy, Massachusetts. Rolling the blood pressure machine next to me, she hooked me up, pulse oximeter on the left index finger and cuff on the upper right arm. Within moments, the alarm sounds filled the room!

"Sir, do you have any cardiac history at all?"

"Yes, ma'am."

"Just lay there. Don't get up. I'll be right back."

Drifting into near unconsciousness, I was drawn back to reality,

"Sir… Sir!" Blasted pesky nurses!

"Yes, ma'am?"

"I need you to take this and try to calm down as much as possible. We're definitely keeping you. This hospital is just an emergency facility now. We're going to have to transfer you to a hospital. We want to help, but where we transfer you to depends on getting control of your vitals. Take this, and just try to stay calm."

Calm? That was easy enough. Let's see, add two days in a storm plus nine-and-a-half hours waiting on a bus, plus thirty hours traveling in a Greyhound, plus 12 more hours combined with a hospital bed, blankets, and pillow? Yeah, you know what that means. I was out like a light in about sixty seconds!

Interrupted again, I wished they would just let me rest!

"Sir, I hate to wake you, but you've been asleep for 18 hours, and I have to get your vital signs."

"We've been monitoring you, but you were so in need of rest, the doctor told us to let you sleep."

As I groggily sat up in bed, the nurse strapped me to the machine, and the alarms began clanging again. My blood pressure was 160/135, and my resting heart rate was 153. These results were after the medication from the night before and eighteen hours of sleep.

For those who do not know, my resting heart rate should've been around 70 bpm and blood pressure about 120/80. As it stood, my blood pressure was dangerously high, but my heart rate was catastrophically high. That was a terrible combination. At my age, the highest my heart rate should be in any situation is in the neighborhood of 167 (220 minus my age). A trip to the bathroom would have elevated my heart above that. The nurse, while trying to reassure me—no panic allowed—called for the doctor. The doctor's clinical diagnosis was "bad shape!" They had other words, but that'll work for here.

"We've got to get both down and quickly!" the doctor declared, after which I was duly shot and pilled.

"You came here for help, and we're going to give you that, but we cannot transport you the way things are."

Even with the previous meetings with God and His promise to me, I was concerned. I will not tell a lie. When a doctor is handling you with kid gloves, and everybody else is running around with concerned looks abounding, it's next to impossible to maintain one's composure.

Every few minutes, the nurse would check my stats. Medication doing its job, we watched the numbers begin to drop. My vitals got to 140/100 at 120 beats per minute and stopped falling.

"I'm afraid to give you any more medication. There may be a delayed effect, and we gave you enough that you should be bottoming out about now. I'm going to deem you safe enough to transport. Your EKG is abnormal, but that fits with your cardiac history. When you get to the hospital, they'll probably dose you again."

He continued after a short pause, "You need to watch this. You were too close to another heart attack. You need to understand this clearly. To hear this is probably stressful, but do not let yourself get stressed out until you get this under control!'"

Visions of the storm danced before my eyes, and I chuckled inwardly. One more evident sign that my Father had everything under control. I hadn't died yet, and He'd told me He had a plan. I trusted Him. Why not? He'd just proved He'd had His hand on my heart the whole time.

The transport gurney rolled in. The ambulance ride to the "full-service" hospital was uneventful.

The doctor was insightful and quick to point out the obvious. I may have been diabetic, and I may have had a definitive cardiac condition, but I, like the physician in front of me, knew those were not at the root of my current issues.

"Looking at your chart, I have to tell you, you are exhibiting classic signs of PTSD. I know nothing about you, but something is going on in your life, and if we do not get a handle on it, it's going to kill you—literally. I don't know how much they told you over in Quincy (pronounced Quinzee, for the uninitiated in Boston-speak), but you were about this close (finger and thumb separated by the thickness of a sheet of paper) to being dead. I don't want you freaking out on me, but you better help me figure this out. I've got you on so much medication right now that some would be in a coma, and yet your heart rate is still above 100 bpm."

"Well, the short answer is I spent close to a year working undercover in Georgia, running about ninety miles an hour, seven days a week, and twenty-four hours a day. I had multiple attempts on my life—one of which broke bones—injuries to my leg, arm and back, concussion, all my teeth kicked down my throat, crushed my left hand, and they kept kicking until they heard sirens coming down the road. Thank God I don't remember most of it, but I did manage to drive away from the ordeal, although I don't remember that part."

He stared at me for a full minute discerning the truth of the matter.

"Well, that would certainly do it! You're going to need some help with that. Your best answer is going to be therapy. You're going to have to work your way back out of this psychological hole. And it's going to take real work. I will keep you here as long as you want to stay, and I'll help you find a therapist when you leave. We're not set up for that here, and I highly recommend some type of medication at least until you leave, so I'm prescribing it. Taking it is your choice, but you won't make it without it. I cannot stress how important this is to your very survival."

Two days into my stay, everything in the hospital was a complete blur. I don't know if the meds were helping or not. I was never awake long enough to tell.

"Look, Doc., I can't do this. I'm never conscious. I'll be asleep again in five minutes."

"Too heavy for you? We can adjust the dosage down, but you're on an extremely light dose."

"I'm already only taking half of what you prescribed."

"Has it occurred to you that your exhaustion is playing a part in this? I don't know everything, obviously, but from the little you told me, it could be many months before you're even close to recovery. The meds are leveling out some of your neurotransmitters that have gone haywire. It's going to take some time to heal. You need to forget some of the things you've gone through. You shouldn't worry so much about the future. That'll take care of itself."

He continued, "Have you given any real consideration to just enjoying each moment you live? Relax. Personal growth isn't always about tomorrow. More often than not, it is about filling up your days in ways that help you move forward, but it is not about where you'll be, it's about where you are. It's about the moments in which you live. Grab each moment and wring your life out of it!"

I smiled as I said, "Somebody told me all that just a couple days ago."

"Really? Who?"

"You'd probably not believe me."

"Must be pretty smart."

"You have no idea. At any rate, I'm stopping the psych meds. I can't think. I can't stay awake. I can't function. I'll take the rest of the medications, but I'm dropping those."

I walked out of the little room and back into my room, laid down, and woke up twenty hours later. I had to admit it, but maybe I was just beyond exhaustion.

But now I was awake. I still wasn't ready for my usual limited sleep of four hours a night but being awake in the hospital was for the birds! It was Monday afternoon.

Ironically, exactly eight days to the minute from when I left Griffin, Georgia, seeking escape and freedom, I was talking to my nurse about escaping the hospital, and she was doing her best to talk me out of it,

"David, you can barely stand on your feet. You need several more days at least."

"I'm feeling trapped. I'm about as nervous as I can be. I'm about to go crazy in here." That last one is kinda funny considering I was voluntarily in a psych ward. One might argue I'd already arrived at crazy, but I digress.

"Well, you don't need to go anywhere today. You have nowhere to go. Stay tonight and talk to your doctor in the morning."

"I'm not trying to argue. I'm just ready to go. Of course, I can wait 'til the morning." Better sense had briefly seized my mind. I grabbed a newspaper crossword puzzle, laid down on my bed to do it, and promptly fell asleep before I answered the first one. A nurse came by, took the pen and paper from my hands, and laid them on my nightstand. I awoke twelve hours later. Hardheaded and stubborn to my detriment? Absolutely! That's still somewhat true, although I have gotten considerably better since then.

I was chompin' at the bit by the time my doctor rolled in.

"David, I told you that you could leave when you're ready. I think you're far from ready. Would you consider a few more days?"

"No."

He looked expectantly at me, obviously hoping for something more.

Look, I'm the consummate salesman. I used to train salespeople, and I was pretty good at it. There are twenty different ways to handle every objection. I can manipulate words with the best of them and sway the opinions of most. Objections are reasons not to do something that could be satisfied.

Someone might say, "I don't have the money right now." Answer: "Well, so if I split those payments up or delay your first payment until next month, you can take delivery today?"

Or,

"I don't think that color is right for my kitchen." Answer: "Ma'am, I've obviously failed you. I'm so sorry! We have more colors. Doesn't this look great against your curtains?"

Those were objections. They were merely seeking information they did not have, and I had not provided enough information. The only answer I ever dreaded from a customer was an emphatic "No." "No, but…" I could deal with, but a simple no is a rejection, not an objection. I know the communication rules!

I also know that the first to speak loses, so as my "no" hung alone in the air, I just sat there and smiled at the doctor's expectant face.

Still silently smiling at the doctor, my "no" had finally drifted to the floor.

"Well, uh, okay, let me get your release papers together. Now, David, you're homeless."

All of creation came to a halt. There were those words again, first heard at the QT on Hamilton Mill Parkway back in Georgia.

"You're homeless."

I don't know if the doctor had punched me if it would have hit me with more devastation. It's not that I didn't realize it. There's just

126

something that makes your entire insides shrivel up in despair, hearing those words. I'll not lie. I almost changed my mind about leaving.

"There's no way you can survive outside. You're going to have to go to a shelter. In your release papers, I'll include a list of all the shelters. You'll have to choose one, and we'll get you a ride there."

Preparing to Serve

The doctor left the room, leaving me to worry about where I would go. My reverie was interrupted by a nurse I'd not seen there in my five days of care.

"I understand you're homeless."

Boy, I sure wished people would stop saying that. It drove a stake into my soul with each utterance.

"Yes, ma'am."

"The doctor's going to give you a list of shelters. On second thought, don't even worry about it. Where you need to go is the Salvation Army Shelter in Cambridge. Don't worry about it. I'll handle it."

She bustled out of the room, and about fifteen minutes later, she came back. With her, she brought my official release papers, my current prescriptions, and one brand new one.

"Here is the doctor's order for you to go to the Salvation Army in Cambridge. I'll get you an Uber ride when you're packed up and ready to go."

Of course, part of the beauty of Uber is you don't have to know how to get somewhere. You don't even have to know where you are. That's a good thing because though I'd been to Boston before, I didn't have a clue where Cambridge was, much less where I could find the Salvation Army, Cambridge Corps. My Uber ride dropped me off at the door of the shelter.

"My name is Mark. Let me get you to fill out some paperwork." He was a friendly and wonderfully polite man in the Salvation Army Shelter office.

It is difficult for me to write about this man now pertaining to our first meeting. To me now, he's "Marky-Mark," and I'll always be "Davey-Dave" to him. Was there anyone who would have been a better first contact? I think not! As our nicknames suggest, we became friends. He is everything you'd want him to be in that position—kind, compassionate, a stickler for the rules, but not so much so that he wasn't willing and able to work around issues to help somebody. He is smart with a certain amount of charisma. Everyone loves Mark!

I had a problem because the shelter needed my picture ID. I didn't have one. I had known I would need ID when I left home. I had my birth certificate and my social security card, but I had no picture ID. Mark explained I could go to the Massachusetts RMV and get it the next day. Since I was coming from the hospital, they'd give me a day to get the ID.

The next morning, I was out the door. I went and obtained a bus pass and made my way to the nearest Massachusetts RMV. I strolled into the Watertown Mall and turned the corner to view the ever so typical, in every state I've ever been, long line!

Well, I expected the line. I had almost everything I needed. I had all the paperwork, except the green kind. Someone had told me they thought there was a program to help folks like me get their IDs. I just had to have faith. God didn't bring me this far to drop me! I was bold. I was humble. Everything would be just all right.

Yeah, right! The government was involved. Something was bound to go wrong. I got to the front of the line where a woman was reviewing documents before I would even get to take a number.

"Sir, your birth certificate is not acceptable. It needs a raised stamp on it, and there used to be a program to help with IDs, but the state stopped it."

The look on my face must've matched the sinking action of my heart.

"Sir, maybe they can help you at the help desk." I think she was genuinely concerned for me.

The only problem? I got the same answer at the help desk, who then pushed me up to the onsite manager.

Well, this wasn't going well. I'm pretty familiar with how things work. No's generally get firmer the further up the chain you go, but if there's any hope, you have to ask.

"Father, I need some help here."

No verbal answer, but I'd already figured out that He's more of a doer. More often than not, His actions speak volumes all the books in the world could not contain! So, I waited to talk with the manager."

"Mr. Riordan, they told you the right thing, but let me see what you have, and I'll see if there's anything I can do."

I cringed as I spoke, "Ma'am, I have an additional problem. I don't have the twenty-five dollars either."

She stared for a moment, and then said, "I don't think there's anything I can do anyway. Let me see, and then we'll worry about that."

Forty-five minutes later, I was walking out of the RMV with a Massachusetts ID. I have no idea what all she did, but what I do know is she paid the fee for my ID out of her own pocket! I've seen plenty of miracles in my life, but this one was truly amazing. God has continually put the right people in front of me at the right time. My friends are as amazed as I am. This kind of thing just doesn't happen! There was no schmoozing here, no smooth-talking, just a plea to my Father.

That's right. My Father was involved, and He never fails!

The next thing I needed to do was to have a checkup with a doctor. Housed in the shelter facility is a clinic from a great organization, Healthcare for the Homeless. I signed up to see the PA and waited for my turn. Another soon-to-be friend walked out and called my name.

"My name is Erlinda. The first thing we need to do is to get the ball rolling on getting you covered with insurance. That's one of the things I do."

We talked as she entered my information.

"Wait a minute. Have you lived in Massachusetts before? And how long have you been here?"

It was Wednesday, "Six days, and no ma'am. I've only visited a few years back for work." I had no idea what she was getting at.

"You have insurance," she said, kinda startled. "Oh, I see here. How in the world did you get insurance activated the day you arrived?"

"I have no idea. I answered some questions when I arrived at the hospital that afternoon, but I never officially applied." I had gotten to the hospital at about 2:00 in the afternoon.

"Yes, well, that office closes at four or five o'clock, and it was activated that day. I don't even know what somebody could do to make that happen so quickly, and I know the system. I know it well. Somebody did something for you."

Looking at me differently, Erlinda ushered me in to see my next hero, Deb Sarsen, PA, who became very important to me as the summer wore on.

Track 9: Waves and Winds

Waves and Winds is a reworking of the hymn "Be Still My Soul," written by Katharina von Schlegal in 1697. The words impacted me deeply as they reminded me of the sovereignty of God that brings peace and steadfastness. I felt the need to weave both a sense of hope and desperation throughout the song musically, a reflection of the journey of the Christian experience. Jesus is leading us to Himself, and no matter our circumstances, He knows that our deepest joy is only found in Him.

-Timothy

"My soul, wait in silence for God alone, for my expectation is from Him. He alone is my rock and my salvation, my fortress where I will not be shaken."
Psalm 62:5, 6 (WEB)

May 6, 2018 10:00 a.m.

I contemplated my new life as I sat in the Salvation Army Church on my second Sunday in Massachusetts. I had been here for ten days, and my feet were on the ground, although I wasn't exactly running. The truth is, I should have stayed longer in the hospital, but Father had my back, as He had promised. It was a new world for me. Everything was different.

Oh, I still had issues, but my perspective had changed.

"Son, that new thing you have is called faith, real faith, life-altering faith. It is My gift to you. Seize life. I like what the doctor told you. 'Wring the life out of every moment.' I kinda helped him with that one. I wanted you to remember it. Follow my leading. I've given you the story you've long desired. Write it down. I have some things in store for the rest of your life."

Gently scolding, He continued, "Now, quit daydreaming and listen to the lesson. This one's just for you, and be prepared, I've got something to show you afterward. Talk to the

Majors. They are now your pastors, and they'll not steer you wrong!"

As I tuned into the teaching, Major Tom Babbitt began speaking from Judges 16 from the story of Samson, "And the hair on his head began to grow again." Yep, a message just for me!

I introduced myself to Major Tom Babbitt, and we talked about the possibility of my playing the piano. He told me to keep on coming back.

I did.

It would be a couple of months down the road when Major Bessie told me she'd been praying for a pianist before I would connect the dots. After all, I had a doctor's prescription to go to the Salvation Army Shelter and a free Uber ride there. I was a pianist, and God had once again moved. It was one of those unrecognized miracles. I see them all the time in my life, but rarely when they're happening.

Settling in at the shelter was a challenge all its own, but by the second full week in Massachusetts, I had a library card, secured with my new ID. I found the amply supplied computer room and began to obey the Lord's command,

"Write it down."

As I was penning my story, my brother was reading along as I wrote—you know, that same brother that gave me his last fifteen dollars as I left Griffin, Georgia,

"Dave, the book needs a 'Eureka!' moment near the end."

I just smiled inside. The life I now live is one Eureka moment after another. My Heavenly Father has called me out, set me apart, and He surrounds me daily. My life has changed to Biblical proportions! It has been one miracle after another, and I can't wait to tell you all about it. The next book is almost complete.

****

End Note

At the time of the above events, I did not often recognize what was going on. Isn't that the way it is typically? We rarely appreciate a miracle when it's taking place because we can't see it until later. I was in the middle of God's miraculous hand moving in my life!

Miracles unseen? How many cataclysmic tsunamis missed the Ark while Noah, his family, and the animals were tucked safely within the boat? How many blows, meant to kill, slightly changed trajectory, leaving Paul with yet another testimony? Better yet, didn't the disciples misunderstand the miracle of the crucifixion as it was taking place?

Horror changes to pure joy as we examine this thing called miraculous living. Noah had to endure the flood, Paul the beatings, and our Savior had to overcome the cross and death. Victory always comes in the morning after the darkest of nights!

And we have been made more than conquerors through Christ, Who Himself overcame sin, death, and the grave. If there's nothing to overcome, and if there's nothing to defeat, how can we conquer? If we never faced hardship, would we ever learn of our need for Him? In our quest to fill that need, oh, how much more we find when we rest in Him!

Life often comes at us a million miles an hour, and by necessity, we must face life on life's terms, with complete reliance on God. There is no other successful life strategy!

I'm afraid I've spent far too much of my life sitting inside my own personal Ark, wondering why I have to endure the storm! I've failed to be grateful for all the destructive waves that merely passed by. I have been unable to understand there is an end to the deluge, and the storms are only temporary.

So, for today, not only will I commit to enduring the storm, I will marvel at the waves that pass me by. And, for today, I will bask in the promise of coming sunlight. On this, it is faith. It is the sure knowledge there is an end, for I have been promised an Abundant Life by One Who never lies!

It is good I boast of my trials, for in those trials, I find patience, the knowledge that experience brings, and hope built upon all of that. It is this hope that cannot be restrained. It resonates with those who would hear me, for who is not seeking the Hope of Life? I have become a soda that has been shaken—no, better yet, a volcano that bursts its earthly bonds—a soul that has found relief!

I would be remiss at this point not to proclaim, "Christ made the way. It is yours for the asking!

He is awaiting your call!!"

In Christ Alone,

the Bread

(A Product of the Loving Baker)

****

Track 10: Sound of the Rivers

Every movie needs a great song playing as the credits roll!

Okay, so this isn't a movie, and all the credit goes to our Father in Heaven—no need to roll past that.

Dan and Timothy would whole-heartedly agree.

It has been incredible working with them and many others to produce this work that goes beyond a typical reading experience.

I have repeatedly told people how cool it is to be a part of this. Their response has usually been incredulous. "It's your story. You're not just a part!" My response has been one full of gratefulness, for there would be no stories without the Author and Finisher of our faith.

There would be no music without the Composer of Hearts.

"It is not my story. It is His story!"

And, to Him, I say as this song says,

"Your Majesty is blowing my mind!"

"Your works declare the glory of Your Kingdom and speak of Your might, to make known to the sons of men Your mighty acts and the Glory of the Majesty of Your Kingdom."
Psalm 145:11-12 (NASB)

I found it easy to tell the story of my life during those two days and what came after.

What came before was a different thing, entirely!

What would you do, and how far would you go to save someone you loved from insured self-destruction?

And, who would be crazy enough to try it?

LOOK FOR

the Baker

AVAILABLE SOON!

the Baker

1

How It All Began

"In the beginning, God created…"

Wait, not quite that far back.

In January of 1965, Jerry and Betty Riordan were expecting their fourth child. There was a heightened sense of expectation in the house. Already the parents of three healthy children, Danny, age six, Becky, age four, and Timmy, age two, my parents were excited that they were soon to have a complete perfect American family of two boys and two girls.

Names were chosen, Dad had pulled Becky's baby clothing from storage in the attic of the Marietta, Georgia, semi-rural home in which they lived. Mom, Betty, was prepared. They knew to be ready at a moment's notice because she was not one to have any labor issues. With their first girl, Rebecca, Mom barely made it to the hospital, and then almost gave birth alone in a hospital room because the nurse walked out to check to see if the doctor had arrived yet.

Her bags were packed.

Dad, Jerry, was prepared as well. There would be no delays in getting the love of his life to the hospital. As an up and coming, promising co-manager of a Kroger grocery store, he stayed near the phone as the February due date got closer.

While certainly far from wealthy, God blessed this little family. They lived paycheck to paycheck and, in fact, had moved to a less expensive home that rented for about fifteen dollars a month less, just to survive. They were all healthy, and they were happy. The addition of another girl-child would complete their image of the perfect family.

As you can already tell, I upset the apple cart, so to speak, from the beginning.

February 15, 1965, rolled around, and at about midnight, Mom's labor began. By 2:08 a.m., I had shattered her image of the perfect family because, at 2:07, Dr. P.E. Parker announced, "It's a boy."

My mother's initial response was she was just happy I was healthy. Nothing else mattered. It would be a few minutes before those emotions flooded through my father because in Georgia, at that time, fathers were not only discouraged from being in the delivery room, hospitals barred fathers from the birthing process.

There was the issue of putting the girl-baby clothes back up and finding a name for this child—the latter was kind of important.

Day three of my nameless life progressed just fine for me because, at that point, I didn't care. The change-the-diaper, reload-the-belly, change-the-diaper cycle was all that gave me any rise of concern.

As Mom dutifully and lovingly tended to those seemingly incessant demands from yours truly, my mother's nurse strolled into the room.

"Now, Mrs. Riordan, this baby needs a name!"

"Everybody told me it would be a girl. I carried him like I did my daughter. I have only thought about a girl's name," declared Mom. "I already have two boys. I didn't want another 'stinkin' boy," she smiled at the nurse with a twinkle in her eyes. "I just can't think of a good name."

"Maybe I can help," offered the nurse.

Mom stated firmly, "It has to be a Bible name for the first name."

The nurse gently took me from my mother's arms, "This looks like a little David."

With one fell swoop by a nurse who never saw me again, Mom entrusted me with the name of the one mentioned in the Bible more times than anyone, other than Jesus. He was awesome. As a young man, David killed Goliath with only a sling. He exhibited great spiritual ethos by not raising his hand against God's chosen king, Saul. He, for Heaven's sake (literally), partially designed and collected material for God's Temple for future construction in Jerusalem. He was a hero.

David was also an adulterer and a murderer—a man so tainted with bloodshed God forbade him from physically building the Temple.

In the end, though, he was a man that pursued having a heart like God's. He was a man who knew how to say, "I'm wrong, please forgive me." By being an example of a penitent, he became the ancestor of the One who brought true forgiveness.

"Not fair! Why saddle me with a name that holds so much baggage and responsibility?" Besides, I can think of better fitting, more suitable names for the man that has lived this life of mine. Judas, who betrayed Jesus—Benedict Arnold, who turned on his country through a mixed-up sense of moral priorities—indeed even Adam, who left all humanity in need. Those names fit me far better—certainly not in human magnitude, but then again, let's face it on February 18, 1965, my parents had just burdened me with the name of the man who established a kingdom that has no end.

Wow! Or, should I say,

"Ouch?!"

****

AFTERWORD

What now?

That's the question that stings the heart of every reader finishing a good book.

The answer is most times, unclear.

The majority of us respond to that post-read melancholy by just moving on to the next book.

That's where the Baker is different.

David Riordan's incredible journey—shared through his bright, lively prose—is a testimony not to his grit and determination, but to the faith that carries and sustains him. To its very last word, Riordan's story proclaims: God is real. Christ is near. The Spirit is working in human life.

What now?

"What now?" is to let this truth be yeast in your own life, that trial and adversity may cause you only to rise the more, a beloved child washed in Christ's grace, a vessel of God's Holy Spirit.

"What now?" is the work of life with God.

May you find yourself blessed in His abundance.

Only By Grace,
The Rev. Tom Hathaway

NOTE FROM THE AUTHOR

May 2020, Austin, TX

Most authors design biographical verbal sketches to sell the author. I would instead promote the Author and Finisher of my faith, Jesus Christ, for, without Him, I am nothing.

This story, the Baker, is my life. I am not the Baker, but rather the product of a particular loving Baker. One who made a point of taking the time to knead and bake my spirit to be what He wanted me to be. I am not entirely where He wants me to be yet, for it is the journey that pleases Him as we grow.

Many people tell us, and we assume that getting saved is about our eventual destination. It's not! It is about when and where we are every moment of our existence. It is an expedition, and we will arrive at each moment more complete than we were when we take that journey with Him.

Not to underrate Heaven, it'll be awesome. However, you can begin a remarkable life in the here and now. Talk to the one who made you. He is expectantly awaiting your call.

Thanks to a Heavenly intervention during a Georgia storm in April 2018, it is a great life and very interesting at times, for this man, who the world had given up for lost!

In Christ Alone,

David W. Riordan

ABOUT THE COMPOSERS
Dan Riordan

Dan graduated from Mercer University with a BA in Music Composition. He received his master's from Southwestern Baptist Theological Seminary. Composing music is nothing new for him. He has written and directed musicals and cantatas for the churches he has served for years.

Highly skilled as an instrumentalist, he plays every instrument for his compositions on the Baker Prelude Soundtrack.

Dan has served in ministry for most of his life working with churches in Georgia, Texas, and Alabama. He has served as a minister of music with additional responsibilities of Christian education. Through the years, he has also found great joy in leading children, teens, and adults to learn musical skills that help them express worship and serve as worship leaders.

When not composing or serving through his church in southwest Georgia, Dan and his wife, Laurie, are constructing a tiny house on their property, where he is attempting to grow much of his own food. And, when not talking to his little brother on the phone, he enjoys the freedom of riding his motorcycle and hiking.

For more outstanding music from Dan, go to youtube.com/watch?v=7Ijz6TsOkVk.

Dan may be contacted at
mountainscape7@gmail.com.

Timothy Riordan

After graduating from Liberty University, Timothy passed on the opportunity for a possible recording contract. Instead, he and his wife, Jillian, self-funded a year-long mission trip to Birmingham, England. While there, Timothy and Jillian supported the local church through pastoral care, serving the community and spreading the name and mission of Jesus. He and his band, Atlas Rhoads, also used their music as an avenue of ministry and successfully toured Europe and Israel with their unique sound and message of Jesus Christ.

A lover of Jesus, Timothy now serves as the worship leader of a growing Church in Charlotte, North Carolina, and is working on a new record with his band.

Timothy composed four of the songs on the Baker Prelude soundtrack. The rich tones of his vocals and striking guitar style are unmistakably Timothy. His background as a cellist also influences him, lending to a symphonic sound in his Indie-style compositions. You may find more of His music on Spotify, YouTube, and all other streaming platforms, and you can follow their journey on Instagram, as well, under @AtlasRhoads.

Tell Your Story!

Come to DavidWRiordan.com/Stories or email your story to theBakerandtheBread@gmail.com and share your story. It may get posted to the page.

Share the hope you have found in Christ. The world is literally dying to hear it!!

"The Gospel begins in the Bible and continues in our lives. When we tell our stories, it is like letting someone read the last few pages in a great book that makes them want to see how the story began."

David W. Riordan

Permission for Biblical Quotations

Books from Greentree Publishers

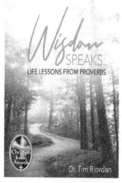

Wisdom Speaks: Life Lessons from Proverbs
By Tim Riordan

Have you ever wished for a "How To" book on life? God has given us one in the book of Proverbs. Join pastor and Bible teacher Dr. Tim Riordan on a journey through this book of wisdom.

Songs from the Heart: Meeting with God in the Psalms
By Tim Riordan

Songs from the Heart is a Bible study/ devotional on the beloved book of Psalms. Dr. Tim Riordan shares insights, Bible teaching and storytelling, making personal application to your life.

When God Promises:
Taking God at His Word Will Free
You from Worry, Stress, & Fear
By Julie McCoy

This six-week study draws on the experiences of people in the Bible who discovered the power of taking God at His word. As you explore their stories you will learn how trusting God's faithfulness to do what He says will give you victory.

Reaching for Life
By Victoria Teague with Connie J. Singleton

Following an eleven-year cocaine addiction and a dangerous career as a dancer in Atlanta's sex industry, Victoria Teague experienced what can only be called a miraculous rescue. After becoming a Christian, Victoria was called not only to share her secrets, but also to spotlight them by ministering to other women in the strip clubs.

The Long Way Home
By Judah Knight

Dive into an adventure of scuba diving, treasure hunting, danger and suspense in Judah Knight's exciting novel, *The Long Way Home.* When Meg was stranded in the Caribbean, her life was changed through an encounter with an old friend that turned into adventure, danger, discovery, and love. Enjoy flinch-free fiction that is safe for the whole family.

Consider other books in the Davenport Series

For more information on any of our publications, visit www.greentreepublishers.com